PROPOSED ROADS TO FREEDOM

SOCIALISM, ANARCHISM AND SYNDICALISM

BY
BERTRAND RUSSELL, F. R. S.

NEW YORK
HENRY HOLT AND COMPANY

192
R96pr

Authorized Edition

~~Brothers College~~

PRINTED IN THE
UNITED STATES OF AMERICA

PREFACE

This book is an attempt to compress into a small compass a discussion which would require many volumes for its adequate treatment. It was completed in April, 1918, in the last days before a period of imprisonment. At that time few would have ventured to prophesy that the fighting would end before the New Year. The coming of peace has made the problems of reconstruction the more urgent. The author has attempted to examine briefly the growth and scope of those pre-war doctrines which aimed at fundamental economic change. These doctrines are considered first historically, then critically, and it is urged that, while none can be accepted *en bloc*, all have something to contribute to the picture of the future society which we should wish to create.

In the historical parts of the work I was much assisted by my friend Mr. Hilderic Cousens, who supplied me with facts on subjects which I had not time to investigate thoroughly myself.

London, January, 1919.

CONTENTS

CHAPTER	PAGE
Introduction	vii

PART I.
HISTORICAL

I. Marx and Socialist Doctrine	1
II. Bakunin and Anarchism	32
III. The Syndicalist Revolt	56

PART II.
PROBLEMS OF THE FUTURE

IV. Work and Pay	86
V. Government and Law	111
VI. International Relations	139
VII. Science and Art Under Socialism	164
VIII. The World as it Could be Made	186

INTRODUCTION

THE attempt to conceive imaginatively a better ordering of human society than the destructive and cruel chaos in which mankind has hitherto existed is by no means modern: it is at least as old as Plato, whose " Republic " set the model for the Utopias of subsequent philosophers. Whoever contemplates the world in the light of an ideal—whether what he seeks be intellect, or art, or love, or simple happiness, or all together—must feel a great sorrow in the evils that men needlessly allow to continue, and—if he be a man of force and vital energy—an urgent desire to lead men to the realization of the good which inspires his creative vision. It is this desire which has been the primary force moving the pioneers of Socialism and Anarchism, as it moved the inventors of ideal commonwealths in the past. In this there is nothing new. What is new in Socialism and Anarchism is that close relation of the ideal to the present sufferings of men, which has enabled powerful political movements to grow out of the hopes of solitary thinkers. It is this that makes Socialism and Anarchism important, and it is this that makes them dangerous to those who batten, consciously or unconsciously upon the evils of our present order of society.

The great majority of men and women, in ordinary times, pass through life without ever contemplating or criticising, as a whole, either their own conditions or those of the world at large. They find themselves born into a certain place in society, and they accept what each day brings forth, without any effort of thought beyond what the immediate present requires. Almost as instinctively as the beasts of the field, they seek the satisfaction of the needs of the moment, without much forethought, and without considering that by sufficient effort the whole conditions of their lives could be changed. A certain percentage, guided by personal ambition, make the effort of thought and will which is necessary to place themselves among the more fortunate members of the community; but very few among these are seriously concerned to secure for all the advantages which they seek for themselves. It is only a few rare and exceptional men who have that kind of love toward mankind at large that makes them unable to endure patiently the general mass of evil and suffering, regardless of any relation it may have to their own lives. These few, driven by sympathetic pain, will seek, first in thought and then in action, for some way of escape, some new system of society by which life may become richer, more full of joy and less full of preventable evils than it is at present. But in the past such men have, as a rule, failed to interest the very victims of the injustices which they wished to remedy. The more unfortunate sections of the population have been ignorant, apathetic from excess of toil and weariness, timorous through the imminent danger of immediate punishment by the holders of power, and morally unreliable owing to the loss of self-respect resulting from their degradation. To create among such classes any conscious, deliberate effort after general amelioration might have seemed a hopeless task, and indeed in the past it has generally proved so. But the modern world, by the increase of education and the rise in the standard of comfort among wage-earners, has produced new conditions, more favorable than ever before to the demand for radical reconstruction. It is above all the Socialists, and in a lesser degree the Anarchists (chiefly as the inspirers of Syndicalism), who have become the exponents of this demand.

What is perhaps most remarkable in regard to both Socialism and Anarchism is the association of a widespread popular movement with ideals for a better world. The ideals have been elaborated, in the first instance, by solitary writers of books, and yet powerful sections of the wage-earning classes have accepted them as their guide in the practical affairs of the world. In regard to Socialism this is evident; but in regard to Anarchism it is only true with some qualification. Anarchism as such has never been a widespread creed; it is only in the modified form of Syndicalism that it has achieved popularity. Unlike Socialism and Anarchism, Syndicalism is primarily the outcome, not of an idea, but of an organization: the fact of Trade Union organization came first, and the ideas of Syndicalism are those which seemed appropriate to this organization in the opinion of the more advanced French Trade Unions. But the ideas are, in the main, derived from Anarchism, and the men who gained acceptance for them were, for the most part, Anarchists. Thus we may regard Syndicalism as the Anarchism of the market-place, as opposed to the Anarchism of isolated individuals which had preserved a precarious life throughout the previous decades. Taking this view, we find in Anarchist-Syndicalism the same combination of ideal and organization as we find in Socialist political parties. It is from this standpoint that our study of these movements will be undertaken.

Socialism and Anarchism, in their modern form, spring respectively from two protagonists, Marx and Bakunin, who fought a lifelong battle, culminating in a split in the first International. We shall begin our study with these two men—first their teaching, and then the organizations which they founded or inspired. This will lead us to the spread of Socialism in more recent years, and thence to the Syndicalist revolt against Socialist emphasis on the State

INTRODUCTION

and political action, and to certain movements outside France which have some affinity with Syndicalism—notably the I. W. W. in America and Guild Socialism in England. From this historical survey we shall pass to the consideration of some of the more pressing problems of the future, and shall try to decide in what respects the world would be happier if the aims of Socialists or Syndicalists were achieved.

My own opinion—which I may as well indicate at the outset—is that pure Anarchism, though it should be the ultimate ideal, to which society should continually approximate, is for the present impossible, and would not survive more than a year or two at most if it were adopted. On the other hand, both Marxian Socialism and Syndicalism, in spite of many drawbacks, seem to me calculated to give rise to a happier and better world than that in which we live. I do not, however, regard either of them as the *best* practicable system. Marxian Socialism, I fear, would give far too much power to the State, while Syndicalism, which aims at abolishing the State, would, I believe, find itself forced to reconstruct a central authority in order to put an end to the rivalries of different groups of producers. The best practicable system, to my mind, is that of Guild Socialism, which concedes what is valid both in the claims of the State Socialists and in the Syndicalist fear of the State, by adopting a system of federalism among trades for reasons similar to those which are recommending federalism among nations. The grounds for these conclusions will appear as we proceed.

Before embarking upon the history of recent movements in favor of radical reconstruction, it will be worth while to consider some traits of character which distinguish most political idealists, and are much misunderstood by the general public for other reasons besides mere prejudice. I wish to do full justice to these reasons, in order to show the more effectually why they ought not to be operative.

The leaders of the more advanced movements are, in general, men of quite unusual disinterestedness, as is evident from a consideration of their careers. Although they have obviously quite as much ability as many men who rise to positions of great power, they do not themselves become the arbiters of contemporary events, nor do they achieve wealth or the applause of the mass of their contemporaries. Men who have the capacity for winning these prizes, and who work at least as hard as those who win them, but deliberately adopt a line which makes the winning of them impossible, must be judged to have an aim in life other than personal advancement; whatever admixture of self-seeking may enter into the detail of their lives, their fundamental motive must be outside Self. The pioneers of Socialism, Anarchism, and Syndicalism have, for the most part, experienced prison, exile, and poverty, deliberately incurred because they would not abandon their propaganda; and by this conduct they have shown that the hope which inspired them was not for themselves, but for mankind.

Nevertheless, though the desire for human welfare is what at bottom determines the broad lines of such men's lives, it often happens that, in the detail of their speech and writing, hatred is far more visible than love. The impatient idealist—and without some impatience a man will hardly prove effective—is almost sure to be led into hatred by the oppositions and disappointments which he encounters in his endeavors to bring happiness to the world. The more certain he is of the purity of his motives and the truth of his gospel, the more indignant he will become when his teaching is rejected. Often he will successfully achieve an attitude of philosophic tolerance as regards the apathy of the masses, and even as regards the whole-hearted opposition of professed defenders of the *status quo*. But the men whom he finds it impossible to forgive are those who profess the same desire for the amelioration of society as he feels himself, but who do not accept his method of achieving this end. The intense faith which enables him to withstand persecution for the sake of his beliefs makes him consider these beliefs so luminously obvious that any thinking man who rejects them must be dishonest, and must be actuated by some sinister motive of treachery to the cause. Hence arises the spirit of the sect, that bitter, narrow orthodoxy which is the bane of those who hold strongly to an unpopular creed. So many real temptations to treachery exist that suspicion is natural. And among leaders, ambition, which they mortify in their choice of a career, is sure to return in a new form: in the desire for intellectual mastery and for despotic power within their own sect. From these causes it results that the advocates of drastic reform divide themselves into opposing schools, hating each other with a bitter hatred, accusing each other often of such crimes as being in the pay of the police, and demanding, of any speaker or writer whom they are to admire, that he shall conform exactly to their prejudices, and make all his teaching minister to their belief that the exact truth is to be found within the limits of their creed. The result of this state of mind is that, to a casual and unimaginative attention, the men who have sacrificed most through the wish to benefit mankind *appear* to be actuated far more by hatred than by love. And the demand for orthodoxy is stifling to any free exercise of intellect. This cause, as well as economic prejudice, has made it difficult for the " intellectuals " to co-operate practically with the more extreme reformers, however they may sympathize with their main purposes and even with nine-tenths of their program.

Another reason why radical reformers are misjudged by ordinary men is that they view existing society from outside, with hostility towards its institutions. Although, for the most part, they have more belief than their neighbors in human nature's inherent capacity for a good life, they are so conscious of the cruelty and oppression resulting from existing institutions that they make a wholly misleading impression of cynicism. Most men have instinctively two entirely different codes of behavior: one toward those whom they regard as companions or colleagues or friends, or in some way members of the same " herd "; the other toward those whom they regard as enemies or outcasts or a danger to society. Radical reformers are apt to concentrate their attention upon the behavior of society toward the latter class, the class of those toward whom the " herd " feels ill-will. This class includes, of course, enemies in war, and criminals; in the minds of those who consider the preservation of the existing order essential to their own safety or privileges, it includes all who advocate any great political or economic change, and all classes which, through their poverty or through any other cause, are likely to feel a dangerous degree of discontent. The ordinary citizen probably seldom thinks about such individuals or classes, and goes through life believing that he and his friends are kindly people, because they have no wish to injure those toward whom they entertain no group-hostility. But the man whose attention is fastened upon the relations of a group with those whom it hates or fears will judge quite differently. In these relations a surprising ferocity is apt to be developed, and a very ugly side of human nature comes to the fore. The opponents of capitalism have learned, through the study of certain historical facts, that this ferocity has often been shown by the capitalists and by the State toward the wage-earning classes, particularly when they have ventured to protest against the unspeakable suffering to which industrialism has usually condemned them. Hence arises a quite different attitude toward existing society from that of the ordinary well-to-do citizen: an attitude as true as his, perhaps also as untrue, but equally based on facts, facts concerning his relations to his enemies instead of to his friends.

The class-war, like wars between nations, produces two opposing views, each equally true and equally untrue. The citizen of a nation at war, when he thinks of his own countrymen, thinks of them primarily as he has experienced them, in dealings with their friends, in their family relations, and so on. They seem to him on the whole kindly, decent folk. But a nation with which his country is at war views his compatriots through the medium of a quite different set of experiences: as they appear in the ferocity of battle, in the invasion and subjugation of a hostile territory, or in the chicanery of a juggling diplomacy. The men of whom these facts are true are the very same as the men whom their compatriots know as husbands or fathers or friends, but they are judged differently because they are judged on different data. And so it is with those who view the capitalist from the standpoint of the revolutionary wage-earner: they appear inconceivably cynical and misjudging to the capitalist, because the facts upon which their view is based are facts which he either does not know or habitually ignores. Yet the view from the outside is just as true as the view from the inside. Both are necessary to the complete truth; and the Socialist, who emphasizes the outside view, is not a cynic, but merely the friend of the wage-earners, maddened by the spectacle of the needless misery which capitalism inflicts upon them.

I have placed these general reflections at the beginning of our study, in order to make it clear to the reader that, whatever bitterness and hate may be found in the movements which we are to examine, it is not bitterness or hate, but love, that is their mainspring. It is difficult not to hate those who torture the objects of our love. Though difficult, it is not impossible; but it requires a breadth of outlook and a comprehensiveness of understanding which are not easy to preserve amid a desperate contest. If ultimate wisdom has not always been preserved by Socialists and Anarchists, they have not differed in this from their opponents; and in the source of their inspiration they have shown themselves superior to those who acquiesce ignorantly or supinely in the injustices and oppressions by which the existing system is preserved.

PROPOSED ROADS TO FREEDOM

SOCIALISM, ANARCHISM AND SYNDICALISM

PART I

HISTORICAL

CHAPTER I

MARX AND SOCIALIST DOCTRINE

SOCIALISM, like everything else that is vital, is rather a tendency than a strictly definable body of doctrine. A definition of Socialism is sure either to include some views which many would regard as not Socialistic, or to exclude others which claim to be included. But I think we shall come nearest to the essence of Socialism by defining it as the advocacy of communal ownership of land and capital. Communal ownership may mean ownership by a democratic State, but cannot be held to include ownership by any State which is not democratic. Communal ownership may also be understood, as Anarchist Communism understands it, in the sense of ownership by the free association of the men and women in a community without those compulsory powers which are necessary to constitute a State. Some Socialists expect communal ownership to arrive suddenly and completely by a catastrophic revolution, while others expect it to come gradually, first in one industry, then in another. Some insist upon the necessity of completeness in the acquisition of land and capital by the public, while others would be content to see lingering islands of private ownership, provided they were not too extensive or powerful. What all forms have in common is democracy and the abolition, virtual or complete, of the present capitalistic system. The distinction between Socialists, Anarchists and Syndicalists turns largely upon the kind of democracy which they desire. Orthodox Socialists are content with parliamentary democracy in the sphere of government, holding that the evils apparent in this form of constitution at present would disappear with the disappearance of capitalism. Anarchists and Syndicalists, on the other hand, object to the whole parliamentary machinery, and aim at a different method of regulating the political affairs of the community. But all alike are democratic in the sense that they aim at abolishing every kind of privilege and every kind of artificial inequality: all alike are champions of the wage-earner in existing society. All three also have much in common in their economic doctrine. All three regard capital and the wages system as a means of exploiting the laborer in the interests of the possessing classes, and hold that communal ownership, in one form or another, is the only means of bringing freedom to the producers. But within the framework of this common doctrine there are many divergences, and even among those who are strictly to be called Socialists, there is a very considerable diversity of schools.

Socialism as a power in Europe may be said to begin with Marx. It is true that before his time there were Socialist theories, both in England and in France. It is also true that in France, during the revolution of 1848, Socialism for a brief period acquired considerable influence in the State. But the Socialists who preceded Marx tended to indulge in Utopian dreams and failed to found any strong or stable political party. To Marx, in collaboration with Engels, are due both the formulation of a coherent body of Socialist doctrine, sufficiently true or plausible to dominate the minds of vast numbers of men, and the formation of the International Socialist movement, which has continued to grow in all European countries throughout the last fifty years.

In order to understand Marx's doctrine, it is necessary to know something of the influences which formed his outlook. He was born in 1818 at Treves in the Rhine Provinces, his father being a legal official, a Jew who had nominally accepted Christianity. Marx studied jurisprudence, philosophy, political economy and history at various German universities. In philosophy he imbibed the doctrines of Hegel, who was then at the height of his fame, and something of these doctrines dominated his thought throughout his life. Like Hegel, he saw in history the development of an Idea. He conceived the changes in the world as forming a logical development, in which one phase passes by revolution into another, which is its antithesis—a conception which gave to his views a certain hard abstractness, and a belief in revolution rather than evolution. But of Hegel's more definite doctrines Marx retained nothing after his youth. He was recognized as a brilliant student, and might have had a prosperous career as a professor or an official, but his interest in politics and his Radical views led him into more arduous paths. Already in 1842 he became editor of a newspaper, which was suppressed by the Prussian Government early in the following year on account of its advanced opinions. This led Marx to go to Paris, where he became known as a Socialist and acquired a knowledge of his French predecessors.[1] Here in the

---

[1] Chief among these were Fourier and Saint-Simon, who constructed somewhat fantastic Socialistic ideal commonwealths. Proudhon, with whom Marx had some not wholly friendly relations, is to be regarded as a forerunner of the Anarchists rather than of orthodox Socialism.

year 1844 began his lifelong friendship with Engels, who had been hitherto in business in Manchester, where he had become acquainted with English Socialism and had in the main adopted its doctrines.[1] In 1845 Marx was expelled from Paris and went with Engels to live in Brussels. There he formed a German Working Men's Association and edited a paper which was their organ. Through his activities in Brussels he became known to the German Communist League in Paris, who, at the end of 1847, invited him and Engels to draw up for them a manifesto, which appeared in January, 1848. This is the famous "Communist Manifesto," in which for the first time Marx's system is set forth. It appeared at a fortunate moment. In the following month, February, the revolution broke out in Paris, and in March it spread to Germany. Fear of the revolution led the Brussels Government to expel Marx from Belgium, but the German revolution made it possible for him

---

[1] Marx mentions the English Socialists with praise in "The Poverty of Philosophy" (1847). They, like him, tend to base their arguments upon a Ricardian theory of value, but they have not his scope or erudition or scientific breadth. Among them may be mentioned Thomas Hodgskin (1787–1869), originally an officer in the Navy, but dismissed for a pamphlet critical of the methods of naval discipline, author of "Labour Defended Against the Claims of Capital" (1825) and other works; William Thompson (1785–1833), author of "Inquiry into the Principles of Distribution of Wealth Most Conducive to Human Happiness" (1824), and "Labour Rewarded" (1825); and Piercy Ravenstone, from whom Hodgskin's ideas are largely derived. Perhaps more important than any of these was Robert Owen.

to return to his own country. In Germany he again edited a paper, which again led him into a conflict with the authorities, increasing in severity as the reaction gathered force. In June, 1849, his paper was suppressed, and he was expelled from Prussia. He returned to Paris, but was expelled from there also. This led him to settle in England—at that time an asylum for friends of freedom—and in England, with only brief intervals for purposes of agitation, he continued to live until his death in 1883.

The bulk of his time was occupied in the composition of his great book, "Capital."[1] His other important work during his later years was the formation and spread of the International Working Men's Association. From 1849 onward the greater part of his time was spent in the British Museum, accumulating, with German patience, the materials for his terrific indictment of capitalist society, but he retained his hold on the International Socialist movement. In several countries he had sons-in-law as lieutenants, like Napoleon's brothers, and in the various internal contests that arose his will generally prevailed.

The most essential of Marx's doctrines may be reduced to three: first, what is called the material-

---

[1] The first and most important volume appeared in 1867: the other two volumes were published posthumously (1885 and 1894).

istic interpretation of history; second, the law of the concentration of capital; and, third, the class-war.

1. *The Materialistic Interpretation of History.*—Marx holds that in the main all the phenomena of human society have their origin in material conditions, and these he takes to be embodied in economic systems. Political constitutions, laws, religions, philosophies—all these he regards as, in their broad outlines, expressions of the economic *régime* in the society that gives rise to them. It would be unfair to represent him as maintaining that the conscious economic motive is the only one of importance; it is rather that economics molds character and opinion, and is thus the prime source of much that appears in consciousness to have no connection with them. He applies his doctrine in particular to two revolutions, one in the past, the other in the future. The revolution in the past is that of the bourgeoisie against feudalism, which finds its expression, according to him, particularly in the French Revolution. The one in the future is the revolution of the wage-earners, or proletariat, against the bourgeoisie, which is to establish the Socialist Commonwealth. The whole movement of history is viewed by him as necessary, as the effect of material causes operating upon human beings. He does not so much advocate the Socialist revolution as predict it. He holds, it is true, that it will be beneficent, but he is much more

concerned to prove that it must inevitably come. The same sense of necessity is visible in his exposition of the evils of the capitalist system. He does not blame capitalists for the cruelties of which he shows them to have been guilty; he merely points out that they are under an inherent necessity to behave cruelly so long as private ownership of land and capital continues. But their tyranny will not last forever, for it generates the forces that must in the end overthrow it.

2. *The Law of the Concentration of Capital.*— Marx pointed out that capitalist undertakings tend to grow larger and larger. He foresaw the substitution of trusts for free competition, and predicted that the number of capitalist enterprises must diminish as the magnitude of single enterprises increased. He supposed that this process must involve a diminution, not only in the number of businesses, but also in the number of capitalists. Indeed, he usually spoke as though each business were owned by a single man. Accordingly, he expected that men would be continually driven from the ranks of the capitalists into those of the proletariat, and that the capitalists, in the course of time, would grow numerically weaker and weaker. He applied this principle not only to industry but also to agriculture. He expected to find the landowners growing fewer and fewer while their estates grew larger and larger. This process

was to make more and more glaring the evils and injustices of the capitalist system, and to stimulate more and more the forces of opposition.

3. *The Class War.*—Marx conceives the wage-earner and the capitalist in a sharp antithesis. He imagines that every man is, or must soon become, wholly the one or wholly the other. The wage-earner, who possesses nothing, is exploited by the capitalists, who possess everything. As the capitalist system works itself out and its nature becomes more clear, the opposition of bourgeoisie and proletariat becomes more and more marked. The two classes, since they have antagonistic interests, are forced into a class war which generates within the capitalist *régime* internal forces of disruption. The working men learn gradually to combine against their exploiters, first locally, then nationally, and at last internationally. When they have learned to combine internationally they must be victorious. They will then decree that all land and capital shall be owned in common; exploitation will cease; the tyranny of the owners of wealth will no longer be possible; there will no longer be any division of society into classes, and all men will be free.

All these ideas are already contained in the "Communist Manifesto," a work of the most amazing vigor and force, setting forth with terse compression the titanic forces of the world, their epic battle, and the inevitable consummation. This work is of such importance in the development of Socialism and gives such an admirable statement of the doctrines set forth at greater length and with more pedantry in "Capital," that its salient passages must be known by anyone who wishes to understand the hold which Marxian Socialism has acquired over the intellect and imagination of a large proportion of working-class leaders.

"A spectre is haunting Europe," it begins, "the spectre of Communism. All the Powers of old Europe have entered into a holy alliance to exorcise this spectre—Pope and Czar, Metternich and Guizot, French Radicals and German police-spies. Where is the party in opposition that has not been decried as communistic by its opponents in power? Where the Opposition that has not hurled back the branding reproach of Communism against the more advanced opposition parties, as well as against its re-actionary adversaries?"

The existence of a class war is nothing new: "The history of all hitherto existing society is the history of class struggles." In these struggles the fight "each time ended, either in a revolutionary re-constitution of society at large, or in the common ruin of the contending classes."

"Our epoch, the epoch of the bourgeoisie . . . has simplified the class antagonisms. Society as a whole is more and more splitting up into two great hostile camps, into two great classes directly facing each other: Bourgeoisie and Proletariat." Then follows a history of the fall of feudalism, leading to a description of the bourgeoisie as a revolutionary force. " The bourgeoisie, historically, has played a most revolutionary part." " For exploitation, veiled by religious and political illusions, it has substituted naked, shameless, direct, brutal exploitation." " The need of a constantly expanding market for its products chases the bourgeoisie over the whole surface of the globe." " The bourgeoisie, during its rule of scarce one hundred years, has created more massive and more colossal productive forces than have all preceding generations together." Feudal relations became fetters: " They had to be burst asunder; they were burst asunder. . . . A similar movement is going on before our own eyes." " The weapons with which the bourgeoisie felled feudalism to the ground are now turned against the bourgeoisie itself. But not only has the bourgoisie forged the weapons that bring death to itself; it has also called into existence the men who are to wield those weapons— the modern working class—the proletarians."

The cause of the destitution of the proletariat are then set forth. " The cost of production of a workman is restricted, almost entirely, to the means of subsistence that he requires for his maintenance and for the propagation of his race. But the price of a commodity, and therefore also of labor, is equal to its cost of production. In proportion, therefore, as the repulsiveness of the work increases, the wage decreases. Nay more, in proportion as the use of machinery and diversion of labor increases, in the same proportion the burden of toil also increases."

" Modern industry has converted the little workshop of the patriarchal master into the great factory of the industrial capitalist. Masses of laborers, crowded into the factory, are organized like soldiers. As privates of the industrial army they are placed under the command of a perfect hierarchy of officers and sergeants. Not only are they slaves of the bourgeois class, and of the bourgeois State, they are daily and hourly enslaved by the machine, by the over-looker, and, above all, by the individual bourgeois manufacturer himself. The more openly this despotism proclaims gain to be its end and aim, the more petty, the more hateful, and the more embittering it is."

The Manifesto tells next the manner of growth of the class struggle. "The proletariat goes through various stages of development. With its birth begins its struggle with the bourgeoisie. At first the contest is carried on by individual laborers, then by the workpeople of a factory, then by the operatives of one trade, in one locality, against the individual bourgeois who directly exploits them. They direct their attacks not against the bourgeois conditions of production, but against the instruments of production themselves."

"At this stage the laborers still form an incoherent mass scattered over the whole country, and broken up by their mutual competition. If anywhere they unite to form more compact bodies, this is not yet the consequence of their own active union, but of the union of the bourgeoisie, which class, in order to attain its own political ends, is compelled to set the whole proletariat in motion, and is moreover yet, for a time, able to do so."

"The collisions between individual workmen and individual bourgeois take more and more the character of collisions between two classes. Thereupon the workers begin to form combinations (Trades Unions) against the bourgeois; they club together in order to keep up the rate of wages; they found permanent associations in order to make provision beforehand for these occasional revolts. Here and there the contest breaks out into riots. Now and then the workers are victorious, but only for a time. The real fruit of their battles lies, not in the immediate result, but in the ever-expanding union of the workers. This union is helped on by the improved means of communication that are created by modern industry, and that place the workers of different localities in contact with one another. It was just this contact that was needed to centralize the numerous local struggles, all of the same character, into one national struggle between classes. But every class struggle is a political struggle. And that union, to attain which the burghers of the Middle Ages, with their miserable highways, required centuries, the modern proletarians, thanks to railways, achieve in a few years. This organization of the proletarians into a class, and consequently into a political party, is continually being upset again by the competition between the workers themselves. But it ever rises up again, stronger, firmer, mightier. It compels legislative recognition of particular interests of the workers, by taking advantage of the divisions among the bourgeoisie itself."

"In the conditions of the proletariat, those of old society at large are already virtually swamped. The proletarian is without property; his relation to his wife and children has no longer anything in common with the bourgeois family-relations; modern industrial labor, modern subjection to capital, the same in England as in France, in America as in Germany, has stripped him of every trace of national character. Law, morality, religion, are to him so many bourgeois prejudices, behind which lurk in ambush just as many bourgeois interests. All the preceding classes that got the upper hand, sought to fortify their already acquired status by subjecting society at large to their conditions of appropriation. The proletarians cannot become masters of the productive forces of society, except by abolishing their own previous mode of appropriation, and thereby also every other previous mode of appropriation. They have nothing of their own to secure and to forcify; their mission is to destroy all previous securities for, and insurances of, individual property. All previous historical movements were movements of minorities, or in the interest of minorities. The proletarian movement is the self-conscious, independent movement of the immense majority, in the interest of the immense majority. The proletariat, the lowest stratum of our present society, cannot stir, cannot raise itself up, without the whole superincumbent strata of official society being sprung into the air."

The Communists, says Marx, stand for the proletariat as a whole. They are international. "The Communists are further reproached with desiring to abolish countries and nationality. The working men have no country. We cannot take from them what they have not got."

The immediate aim of the Communists is the conquests of political power by the proletariat. "The theory of the Communists may be summed up in the single sentence: Abolition of private property."

The materialistic interpretation of history is used to answer such charges as that Communism is anti-Christian. "The charges against Communism made from a religious, a philosophical, and, generally, from an ideological standpoint, are not deserving of serious examination. Does it require deep intuition to comprehend that man's ideas, views and conceptions, in one word, man's consciousness, changes with every change in the conditions of his material existence, in his social relations, and in his social life?"

The attitude of the Manifesto to the State is not altogether easy to grasp. "The executive of the modern State," we are told, "is but a Committee for managing the common affairs of the whole bourgeoisie." Nevertheless, the first step for the proletariat must be to acquire control of the State. "We have seen above, that the first step in the revolution by the working class, is to raise the proletariat to the position of ruling class, to win the battle of democracy. The proletariat will use its political supremacy to wrest, by degrees, all capital from the bourgeoisie, to centralize all instruments of production in the hands of the State, *i.e.*, of the proletariat organized as the ruling class; and to increase the total of productive forces as rapidly as possible."

MARX AND SOCIALIST DOCTRINE   17

The Manifesto passes on to an immediate program of reforms, which would in the first instance much increase the power of the existing State, but it is contended that when the Socialist revolution is accomplished, the State, as we know it, will have ceased to exist. As Engels says elsewhere, when the proletariat seizes the power of the State " it puts an end to all differences of class and antagonisms of class, and consequently also puts an end to the State as a State." Thus, although State Socialism might, in fact, be the outcome of the proposals of Marx and Engels, they cannot themselves be accused of any glorification of the State.

The Manifesto ends with an appeal to the wage-earners of the world to rise on behalf of Communism. " The Communists disdain to conceal their views and aims. They openly declare that their ends can be attained only by the forcible overthrow of all existing social conditions. Let the ruling classes tremble at a Communistic revolution. The proletarians have nothing to lose but their chains. They have a world to win. Working men of all countries, unite!"

In all the great countries of the Continent, except Russia, a revolution followed quickly on the publication of the Communist Manifesto, but the revolution was not economic or international, except at first in France. Everywhere else it was inspired by the ideas of nationalism. Accordingly, the rulers of the world, momentarily terrified, were able to recover power by fomenting the enmities inherent in the nationalist idea, and everywhere, after a very brief triumph, the revolution ended in war and reaction. The ideas of the Communist Manifesto appeared before the world was ready for them, but its authors lived to see the beginnings of the growth of that Socialist movement in every country, which has pressed on with increasing force, influencing Governments more and more, dominating the Russian Revolution, and perhaps capable of achieving at no very distant date that international triumph to which the last sentences of the Manifesto summon the wage-earners of the world.

Marx's *magnum opus*, " Capital," added bulk and substance to the theses of the Communist Manifesto. It contributed the theory of surplus value, which professed to explain the actual mechanism of capitalist exploitation. This doctrine is very complicated and is scarcely tenable as a contribution to pure theory. It is rather to be viewed as a translation into abstract terms of the hatred with which Marx regarded the system that coins wealth out of human lives, and it is in this spirit, rather than in that of disinterested analysis, that it has been read by its admirers. A critical examination of the theory of surplus value would require much difficult and abstract discussion of pure economic theory without having much bearing upon the practical truth or falsehood of Socialism; it has therefore seemed impossible within the limits of the present volume. To my mind the best parts of the book are those which deal with economic facts, of which Marx's knowledge was encyclopædic. It was by these facts that he hoped to instil into his disciples that firm and undying hatred that should make them soldiers to the death in the class war. The facts which he accumulates are such as are practically unknown to the vast majority of those who live comfortable lives. They are very terrible facts, and the economic system which generates them must be acknowledged to be a very terrible system. A few examples of his choice of facts will serve to explain the bitterness of many Socialists:—

Mr. Broughton Charlton, county magistrate, declared, as chairman of a meeting held at the Assembly Rooms, Nottingham, on the 14th January, 1860, "that there was an amount of privation and suffering among that portion of the population connected with the lace trade, unknown in other parts of the kingdom, indeed, in the civilized world. . . . Children of nine or ten years are dragged from their squalid beds at two, three, or four o'clock in the morning and compelled to work for a bare subsistence until ten, eleven, or twelve at night, their limbs wearing away, their frames dwindling, their faces whitening, and their humanity absolutely sinking into a stone-like torpor, utterly horrible to contemplate."[1]

Three railway men are standing before a London coroner's jury—a guard, an engine-driver, a signalman. A tremendous railway accident has hurried hundreds of passengers into another world. The negligence of the employés is the cause of the misfortune. They declare with one voice before the jury that ten or twelve years before, their labor only lasted eight hours a day. During the last five or six years it had been screwed up to 14, 18, and 20 hours, and under a specially severe pressure of holiday-makers, at times of excursion trains, it often lasted 40 or 50 hours without a break. They were ordinary men, not Cyclops. At a certain point their labor-power failed. Torpor seized them. Their brain ceased to think, their eyes to see. The thoroughly "respectable" British jurymen answered by a verdict that sent them to the next assizes on a charge of manslaughter, and, in a gentle "rider" to their verdict, expressed the pious hope that the capitalistic magnates of the railways would, in future, be more extravagant in the purchase of a sufficient quantity of labor-power, and more "abstemious," more "self-denying," more "thrifty," in the draining of paid labor-power.[2]

In the last week of June, 1863, all the London daily papers published a paragraph with the "sensational" heading, "Death from simple over-work." It dealt with the death of the milliner, Mary Anne Walkley, 20 years of age, employed in a highly respectable dressmaking

---
[1] Vol. i, p. 227.
[2] Vol. i, pp. 237, 238.

establishment, exploited by a lady with the pleasant name of Elise. The old, often-told story was once more recounted. This girl worked, on an average, 16½ hours, during the season often 30 hours, without a break, whilst her failing labor-power was revived by occasional supplies of sherry, port, or coffee. It was just now the height of the season. It was necessary to conjure up in the twinkling of an eye the gorgeous dresses for the noble ladies bidden to the ball in honor of the newly-imported Princess of Wales. Mary Anne Walkley had worked without intermission for 26½ hours, with 60 other girls, 30 in one room, that only afforded 1/3 of the cubic feet of air required for them. At night, they slept in pairs in one of the stifling holes into which the bedroom was divided by partitions of board. And this was one of the best millinery establishments in London. Mary Anne Walkley fell ill on the Friday, died on Sunday, without, to the astonishment of Madame Elise, having previously completed the work in hand. The doctor, Mr. Keys, called too late to the death bed, duly bore witness before the coroner's jury that "Mary Anne Walkley had died from long hours of work in an overcrowded workroom, and a too small and badly ventilated bedroom." In order to give the doctor a lesson in good manners, the coroner's jury thereupon brought in a verdict that "the deceased had died of apoplexy, but there was reason to fear that her death had been accelerated by over-work in an over-crowded workroom, &c." "Our white slaves," cried the "Morning Star," the organ of the free-traders, Cobden and Bright, "our white slaves, who are toiled into the grave, for the most part silently pine and die."[1]

Edward VI: A statue of the first year of his reign, 1547, ordains that if anyone refuses to work, he shall be condemned as a slave to the person who has denounced him as an idler. The master shall feed his slave on bread and water, weak broth and such refuse meat as he thinks fit. He has the right to force him to do any work, no matter how disgusting, with whip and chains. If the slave is absent a fortnight, he is condemned to slavery for life and is to be branded on forehead or back with the letter S; if he runs away thrice, he is to be executed as a felon. The master can sell him, bequeath him, let him out on hire as a slave, just as any other personal chattel or cattle. If the slaves attempt anything against the masters, they are also to be executed. Justices of the peace, on information, are to hunt the rascals down. If it happens that a vagabond has been idling about for three days, he is to be taken to his birthplace, branded with a redhot iron with the letter V on the breast and be set to work, in chains, in the streets or at some other labor. If the vagabond gives a false birthplace, he is then to become the slave for life of this place, of its inhabitants, or its corporation, and to be branded with an S. All persons have the right to take away the children of the vagabonds and to keep them as apprentices, the young men until the 24th year, the girls until the 20th. If they run away, they are to become up to this age the slaves of their masters, who can put them in irons, whip

---

[1] Vol. i, pp. 239, 240.

them, &c., if they like. Every master may put an iron ring around the neck, arms or legs of his slave, by which to know him more easily and to be more certain of him. The last part of this statute provides that certain poor people may be employed by a place or by persons, who are willing to give them food and drink and to find them work. This kind of parish-slaves was kept up in England until far into the 19th century under the name of "roundsmen."[1]

Page after page and chapter after chapter of facts of this nature, each brought up to illustrate some fatalistic theory which Marx professes to have proved by exact reasoning, cannot but stir into fury any passionate working-class reader, and into unbearable shame any possessor of capital in whom generosity and justice are not wholly extinct.

Almost at the end of the volume, in a very brief chapter, called "Historical Tendency of Capitalist Accumulation," Marx allows one moment's glimpse of the hope that lies beyond the present horror:—

As soon as this process of transformation has sufficiently decomposed the old society from top to bottom, as soon as the laborers are turned into proletarians, their means af labor into capital, as soon as the capitalist mode of production stands on its own feet, then the further socialization of labor and further transformation of the land and other means of production into so-

[1] Vol. i, pp. 758, 759.

cially exploited and, therefore, common means of production, as well as the further expropriation of private proprietors, takes a new form. That which is now to be expropriated is no longer the laborer working for himself, but the capitalist exploiting many laborers. This expropriation is accomplished by the action of the immanent laws of capitalistic production itself, by the centralization of capital. One capitalist always kills many, and in hand with this centralization, or this expropriation of many capitalists by few, develop, on an ever extending scale, the co-operative form of the labor-process, the conscious technical application of science, the methodical cultivation of the soil, the transformation of the instruments of labor into instruments of labor only usable in common, the economizing of all means of production by their use as the means of production of combined, socialized labor, the entanglement of all peoples in the net of the world-market, and with this, the international character of the capitalistic régime. Along with the constantly diminishing number of the magnates of capital, who usurp and monopolize all advantages of this process of transformation, grows the mass of misery, oppression, slavery, degradation, exploitation; but with this, too, grows the revolt of the working-class, a class always increasing in numbers, and disciplined, united, organized by the very mechanism of the process of capitalist production itself. The monopoly of capital becomes a fetter upon the mode of production, which has sprung up and flourished along with, and under it. Centralization of the means of production and socialization of labor at last reach a point where they

MARX AND SOCIALIST DOCTRINE 25

become incompatible with their capitalist integument. This integument is burst asunder. The knell of capitalist private property sounds. The expropriators are expropriated,[1]

That is all. Hardly another word from beginning to end is allowed to relieve the gloom, and in this relentless pressure upon the mind of the reader lies a great part of the power which this book has acquired.

Two questions are raised by Marx's work: First, Are his laws of historical development true? Second, Is Socialism desirable? The second of these questions is quite independent of the first. Marx professes to prove that Socialism *must* come, but scarcely concerns himself to argue that when it comes it will be a good thing. It may be, however, that if it comes, it will be a good thing, even though all Marx's arguments to prove that it must come should be at fault. In actual fact, time has shown many flaws in Marx's theories. The development of the world has been sufficiently like his prophecy to prove him a man of very unusual penetration, but has not been sufficiently like to make either political or economic history exactly such as he predicted that it would be. Nationalism, so far from diminishing, has increased, and has failed to be conquered by the cosmopolitan

---

[1] Vol i, pp. 788, 789.

tendencies which Marx rightly discerned in finance. Although big businesses have grown bigger and have over a great area reached the stage of monopoly, yet the number of shareholders in such enterprises is so large that the actual number of individuals interested in the capitalist system has continually increased. Moreover, though large firms have grown larger, there has been a simultaneous increase in firms of medium size. Meanwhile the wage-earners, who were, according to Marx, to have remained at the bare level of subsistence at which they were in the England of the first half of the nineteenth century, have instead profited by the general increase of wealth, though in a lesser degree than the capitalists. The supposed iron law of wages has been proved untrue, so far as labor in civilized countries is concerned. If we wish now to find examples of capitalist cruelty analogous to those with which Marx's book is filled, we shall have to go for most of our material to the Tropics, or at any rate to regions where there are men of inferior races to exploit. Again: the skilled worker of the present day is an aristocrat in the world of labor. It is a question with him whether he shall ally himself with the unskilled worker against the capitalist, or with the capitalist against the unskilled worker. Very often he is himself a capitalist in a small way, and if he is not so individually, his trade union or his friendly society is pretty sure to be so. Hence the sharpness of the class war has not been maintained. There are gradations, intermediate ranks between rich and poor, instead of the clear-cut logical antithesis between the workers who have nothing and the capitalists who have all. Even in Germany, which became the home of orthodox Marxianism and developed a powerful Social-Democratic party, nominally accepting the doctrine of " Das Kapital " as all but verbally inspired, even there the enormous increase of wealth in all classes in the years preceding the war led Socialists to revise their beliefs and to adopt an evolutionary rather than a revolutionary attitude. Bernstein, a German Socialist who lived long in England, inaugurated the " Revisionist " movement which at last conquered the bulk of the party. His criticisms of Marxian orthodoxy are set forth in his " Evolutionary Socialism."[1] Bernstein's work, as is common in Broad Church writers, consists largely in showing that the Founders did not hold their doctrines so rigidly as their followers have done. There is much in the writings of Marx and Engels that cannot be fitted into the rigid orthodoxy which grew up among their disciples. Bernstein's

---

[1] " Die Voraussetzungen des Sozialismus und die Aufgaben der Sozial-Demokratie."
In March, 1914, Bernstein delivered a lecture in Budapest, in which he withdrew from several of the positions he had taken up (vide Budapest "Volksstimme," March 19, 1914).

main criticisms of these disciples, apart from such as we have already mentioned, consist in a defense of piecemeal action as against revolution. He protests against the attitude of undue hostility to Liberalism which is common among Socialists, and he blunts the edge of the Internationalism which undoubtedly is part of the teachings of Marx. The workers, he says, have a Fatherland as soon as they become citizens, and on this basis he defends that degree of nationalism which the war has since shown to be prevalent in the ranks of Socialists. He even goes so far as to maintain that European nations have a right to tropical territory owing to their higher civilization. Such doctrines diminish revolutionary ardor and tend to transform Socialists into a left wing of the Liberal Party. But the increasing prosperity of wage-earners before the war made these developments inevitable. Whether the war will have altered conditions in this respect, it is as yet impossible to know. Bernstein concludes with the wise remark that: " We have to take working men as they are. And they are neither so universally paupers as was set out in the Communist Manifesto, nor so free from prejudices and weaknesses as their courtiers wish to make us believe."

Berstein represents the decay of Marxian orthodoxy from within. Syndicalism represents an attack against it from without, from the standpoint of a doctrine which professes to be even more radical and more revolutionary than that of Marx and Engels. The attitude of Syndicalists to Marx may be seen in Sorel's little book, "La Décomposition du Marxisme," and in his larger work, "Reflections on Violence," authorized translation by T. E. Hulme (Allen & Unwin, 1915). After quoting Bernstein, with approval in so far as he criticises Marx, Sorel proceeds to other criticisms of a different order. He points out (what is true) that Marx's theoretical economics remain very near to Manchesterism: the orthodox political economy of his youth was accepted by him on many points on which it is now known to be wrong. According to Sorel, the really essential thing in Marx's teaching is the class war. Whoever keeps this alive is keeping alive the spirit of Socialism much more truly than those who adhere to the letter of Social-Democratic orthodoxy. On the basis of the class war, French Syndicalists developed a criticism of Marx which goes much deeper than those that we have been hitherto considering. Marx's views on historical development may have been in a greater or less degree mistaken in fact, and yet the economic and political system which he sought to create might be just as desirable as his followers suppose. Syndicalism, however, criticises, not only Marx's views of fact, but also the goal at which he aims and the general nature of the means which he recommends. Marx's ideas were formed at a time when democracy did not yet exist. It was in the very year in which "Das Kapital" appeared that urban working men first got the vote in England and universal suffrage was granted by Bismarck in Northern Germany. It was natural that great hopes should be entertained as to what democracy would achieve. Marx, like the orthodox economists, imagined that men's opinions are guided by a more or less enlightened view of economic self-interest, or rather of economic class interest. A long experience of the workings of political democracy has shown that in this respect Disraeli and Bismarck were shrewder judges of human nature than either Liberals or Socialists. It has become increasingly difficult to put trust in the State as a means to liberty, or in political parties as instruments sufficiently powerful to force the State into the service of the people. The modern State, says Sorel, "is a body of intellectuals, which is invested with privileges, and which possesses means of the kind called political for defending itself against the attacks made on it by other groups of intellectuals, eager to possess the profits of public employment. Parties are constituted in order to acquire the conquest of these employments, and they are analogous to the State."[1]

Syndicalists aim at organizing men, not by party,

---
[1] La Décomposition du Marxisme," p. 53.

MARX AND SOCIALIST DOCTRINE 31

but by occupation. This, they say, alone represents the true conception and method of the class war. Accordingly they despise all *political* action through the medium of Parliament and elections: the kind of action that they recommend is direct action by the revolutionary syndicate or trade union. The battle-cry of industrial versus political action has spread far beyond the ranks of French Syndicalism. It is to be found in the I. W. W. in America, and among Industrial Unionists and Guild Socialists in Great Britain. Those who advocate it, for the most part, aim also at a different goal from that of Marx. They believe that there can be no adequate individual freedom where the State is all-powerful, even if the State be a Socialist one. Some of them are out-and-out Anarchists, who wish to see the State wholly abolished; others only wish to curtail its authority. Owing to this movement, opposition to Marx, which from the Anarchist side existed from the first, has grown very strong. It is this opposition in its older form that will occupy us in our next chapter.

CHAPTER II

BAKUNIN AND ANARCHISM

In the popular mind, an Anarchist is a person who throws bombs and commits other outrages, either because he is more or less insane, or because he uses the pretense of extreme political opinions as a cloak for criminal proclivities. This view is, of course, in every way inadequate. Some Anarchists believe in throwing bombs; many do not. Men of almost every other shade of opinion believe in throwing bombs in suitable circumstances: for example, the men who threw the bomb at Sarajevo which started the present war were not Anarchists, but Nationalists. And those Anarchists who are in favor of bomb-throwing do not in this respect differ on any vital principle from the rest of the community, with the exception of that infinitesimal portion who adopt the Tolstoyan attitude of non-resistance. Anarchists, like Socialists, usually believe in the doctrine of the class war, and if they use bombs, it is as Governments use bombs, for purposes of war: but for every bomb manufactured by an Anarchist, many millions are manufactured by Governments, and for every man killed by Anarchist violence, many millions are killed by the violence of States. We may, therefore, dismiss from our minds the whole question of violence, which plays so large a part in the popular imagination, since it is neither essential nor peculiar to those who adopt the Anarchist position.

Anarchism, as its derivation indicates, is the theory which is opposed to every kind of forcible government. It is opposed to the State as the embodiment of the force employed in the government of the community. Such government as Anarchism can tolerate must be free government, not merely in the sense that it is that of a majority, but in the sense that it is that assented to by all. Anarchists object to such institutions as the police and the criminal law, by means of which the will of one part of the community is forced upon another part. In their view, the democratic form of government is not very enormously preferable to other forms so long as minorities are compelled by force or its potentiality to submit to the will of majorities. Liberty is the supreme good in the Anarchist creed, and liberty is sought by the direct road of abolishing all forcible control over the individual by the community.

Anarchism, in this sense, is no new doctrine. It is set forth admirably by Chuang Tzu, a Chinese philosopher, who lived about the year 300 B. C.:—

Horses have hoofs to carry them over frost and snow; hair, to protect them from wind and cold. They eat grass and drink water, and fling up their heels over the champaign. Such is the real nature of horses. Palatial dwellings are of no use to them.

One day Po Lo appeared, saying: " I understand the management of horses."

So he branded them, and clipped them, and pared their hoofs, and put halters on them, tying them up by the head and shackling them by the feet, and disposing them in stables, with the result that two or three in every ten died. Then he kept them hungry and thirsty, trotting them and galloping them, and grooming, and trimming, with the misery of the tasselled bridle before and the fear of the knotted whip behind, until more than half of them were dead.

The potter says: " I can do what I will with clay. If I want it round, I use compasses; if rectangular, a square."

The carpenter says: " I can do what I will with wood. If I want it curved, I use an arc; if straight, a line."

But on what grounds can we think that the natures of clay and wood desire this application of compasses and square, of arc and line? Nevertheless, every age extols Po Lo for his skill in managing horses, and potters and carpenters for their skill with clay and wood. Those who *govern* the empire make the same mistake.

Now I regard government of the empire from quite a different point of view.

BAKUNIN AND ANARCHISM

The people have certain natural instincts:—to weave and clothe themselves, to till and feed themselves. These are common to all humanity, and all are agreed thereon. Such instincts are called "Heaven-sent."

And so in the days when natural instincts prevailed, men moved quietly and gazed steadily. At that time there were no roads over mountains, nor boats, nor bridges over water. All things were produced, each for its own proper sphere. Birds and beasts multiplied; trees and shrubs grew up. The former might be led by the hand; you could climb up and peep into the raven's nest. For then man dwelt with birds and beasts, and all creation was one. There were no distinctions of good and bad men. Being all equally without knowledge, their virtue could not go astray. Being all equally without evil desires, they were in a state of natural integrity, the perfection of human existence.

But when Sages appeared, tripping up people over charity and fettering them with duty to their neighbor. doubt found its way into the world. And then, with their gushing over music and fussing over ceremony, the empire became divided against itself.[1]

The modern Anarchism, in the sense in which we shall be concerned with it, is associated with belief in the communal ownership of land and capital, and is thus in an important respect akin to Socialism. This doctrine is properly called Anarchist Com-

---
[1] "Musings of a Chinese Mystic." Selections from the Philosophy of Chuang Tzu. With an Introduction by Lionel Giles, M.A. (Oxon.). Wisdom of the East Series, John Murray, 1911. Pages 66-68.

munism, but as it embraces practically all modern Anarchism, we may ignore individualist Anarchism altogether and concentrate attention upon the communistic form. Socialism and Anarchist Communism alike have arisen from the perception that private capital is a source of tyranny by certain individuals over others. Orthodox Socialism believes that the individual will become free if the State becomes the sole capitalist. Anarchism, on the contrary, fears that in that case the State might merely inherit the tyrannical propensities of the private capitalist. Accordingly, it seeks for a means of reconciling communal ownership with the utmost possible diminution in the powers of the State, and indeed ultimately with the complete abolition of the State. It has arisen mainly within the Socialist movement as its extreme left wing.

In the same sense in which Marx may be regarded as the founder of modern Socialism, Bakunin may be regarded as the founder of Anarchist Communism. But Bakunin did not produce, like Marx, a finished and systematic body of doctrine. The nearest approach to this will be found in the writings of his follower, Kropotkin. In order to explain modern Anarchism we shall begin with the life of Bakunin[1]

---

[1] An account of the life of Bakunin from the Anarchist standpoint will be found in vol. ii of the complete edition of his works: "Michel Bakounine, Œuvres," Tome II. Avec une notice biographique, des avant-propos et des notes, par James Guillaume. Paris, P.-V, Stock, Éditeur, pp. v-lxiii.

and the history of his conflicts with Marx, and shall then give a brief account of Anarchist theory as set forth partly in his writings, but more in those of Kropotkin.[1]

Michel Bakunin was born in 1814 of a Russian aristocratic family. His father was a diplomatist, who at the time of Bakunin's birth had retired to his country estate in the Government of Tver. Bakunin entered the school of artillery in Petersburg at the age of fifteen, and at the age of eighteen was sent as an ensign to a regiment stationed in the Government of Minsk. The Polish insurrection of 1830 had just been crushed. " The spectacle of terrorized Poland," says Guillaume, " acted powerfully on the heart of the young officer, and contributed to inspire in him the horror of despotism." This led him to give up the military career after two years' trial. In 1834 he resigned his commission and went to Moscow, where he spent six years studying philosophy. Like all philosophical students of that period, he became a Hegelian, and in 1840 he went to Berlin to continue his studies, in the hope of ultimately becoming a professor. But after this time his opinions underwent a rapid change. He found it impossible to accept the Hegelian maxim that whatever is, is rational, and in 1842 he migrated to Dresden, where

---

[1] Criticism of these theories will be reserved for Part II.

he became associated with Arnold Ruge, the publisher of "Deutsche Jahrbuecher." By this time he had become a revolutionary, and in the following year he incurred the hostility of the Saxon Government. This led him to go to Switzerland, where he came in contact with a group of German Communists, but, as the Swiss police importuned him and the Russian Government demanded his return, he removed to Paris, where he remained from 1843 to 1847. These years in Paris were important in the formation of his outlook and opinions. He became acquainted with Proudhon, who exercised a considerable influence on him; also with George Sand and many other well-known people. It was in Paris that he first made the acquaintance of Marx and Engels, with whom he was to carry on a lifelong battle. At a much later period, in 1871, he gave the following account of his relations with Marx at this time:—

Marx was much more advanced than I was, as he remains to-day not more advanced but incomparably more learned than I am. I knew then nothing of political economy. I had not yet rid myself of metaphysical abstractions, and my Socialism was only instinctive. He, though younger than I, was already an atheist, an instructed materialist, a well-considered Socialist. It was just at this time that he elaborated the first foundations of his present system. We saw each other fairly often, for I respected him much for his learning and his passionate and serious devotion (always mixed, however, with personal vanity) to the cause of the proletariat, and I sought eagerly his conversation, which was always instructive and clever, when it was not inspired by a paltry hate, which, alas! happened only too often. But there was never any frank intimacy between us. Our temperaments would not suffer it. He called me a sentimental idealist, and he was right; I called him a vain man, perfidious and crafty, and I also was right.

Bakunin never succeeded in staying long in one place without incurring the enmity of the authorities. In November, 1847, as the result of a speech praising the Polish rising of 1830, he was expelled from France at the request of the Russian Embassy, which, in order to rob him of public sympathy, spread the unfounded report that he had been an agent of the Russian Government, but was no longer wanted because he had gone too far. The French Government, by calculated reticence, encouraged this story, which clung to him more or less throughout his life.

Being compelled to leave France, he went to Brussels, where he renewed acquaintance with Marx. A letter of his, written at this time, shows that he entertained already that bitter hatred for which afterward he had so much reason. "The Germans, artisans, Bornstedt, Marx and Engels—and, above all, Marx—are here, doing their ordinary mischief.

Vanity, spite, gossip, theoretical overbearingness and practical pusillanimity—reflections on life, action and simplicity, and complete absence of life, action and simplicity—literary and argumentative artisans and repulsive coquetry with them: 'Feuerbach is a bourgeois,' and the word 'bourgeois' grown into an epithet and repeated *ad nauseum*, but all of them themselves from head to foot, through and through, provincial bourgeois. With one word, lying and stupidity, stupidity and lying. In this society there is no possibility of drawing a free, full breath. I hold myself aloof from them, and have declared quite decidedly that I will not join their communistic union of artisans, and will have nothing to do with it."

The Revolution of 1848 led him to return to Paris and thence to Germany. He had a quarrel with Marx over a matter in which he himself confessed later that Marx was in the right. He became a member of the Slav Congress in Prague, where he vainly endeavored to promote a Slav insurrection. Toward the end of 1848, he wrote an "Appeal to Slavs," calling on them to combine with other revolutionaries to destroy the three oppressive monarchies, Russia, Austria and Prussia. Marx attacked him in print, saying, in effect, that the movement for Bohemian independence was futile because the Slavs had no future, at any rate in those regions where they happened to be subject to Germany and Austria. Bakunin accused Marx of German patriotism in this matter, and Marx accused him of Pan-Slavism, no doubt in both cases justly. Before this dispute, however, a much more serious quarrel had taken place. Marx's paper, the "Neue Rheinische Zeitung," stated that George Sand had papers proving Bakunin to be a Russian Government agent and one of those responsible for the recent arrest of Poles. Bakunin, of course, repudiated the charge, and George Sand wrote to the "Neue Rheinische Zeitung," denying this statement *in toto*. The denials were published by Marx, and there was a nominal reconciliation, but from this time onward there was never any real abatement of the hostility between these rival leaders, who did not meet again until 1864.

Meanwhile, the reaction had been everywhere gaining ground. In May, 1849, an insurrection in Dresden for a moment made the revolutionaries masters of the town. They held it for five days and established a revolutionary government. Bakunin was the soul of the defense which they made against the Prussian troops. But they were overpowered, and at last Bakunin was captured while trying to escape with Heubner and Richard Wagner, the last of whom, fortunately for music, was not captured.

Now began a long period of imprisonment in many prisons and various countries. Bakunin was

sentenced to death on the 14th of January, 1850, but
his sentence was commuted after five months, and he
was delivered over to Austria, which claimed the
privilege of punishing him. The Austrians, in their
turn, condemned him to death in May, 1851, and
again his sentence was commuted to imprisonment for
life. In the Austrian prisons he had fetters on hands
and feet, and in one of them he was even chained to the
wall by the belt. There seems to have been some
peculiar pleasure to be derived from the punishment
of Bakunin, for the Russian Government in its turn
demanded him of the Austrians, who delivered him
up. In Russia he was confined, first in the Peter and
Paul fortress and then in the Schluesselburg. There
he suffered from scurvy and all his teeth fell out.
His health gave way completely, and he found almost
all food impossible to assimilate. " But, if his body
became enfeebled, his spirit remained inflexible. He
feared one thing above all. It was to find himself
some day led, by the debilitating action of prison,
to the condition of degradation of which Silvio Pellico
offers a well-known type. He feared that he might
cease to hate, that he might feel the sentiment of
revolt which upheld him becoming extinguished in
his heart, that he might come to pardon his perse-
cutors and resign himself to his fate. But this fear
was superfluous; his energy did not abandon him a

BAKUNIN AND ANARCHISM

single day, and he emerged from his cell the same man as when he entered."[1]

After the death of the Tsar Nicholas many political prisoners were amnested, but Alexander II with his own hand erased Bakunin's name from the list. When Bakunin's mother succeeded in obtaining an interview with the new Tsar, he said to her, " Know, Madame, that so long as your son lives, he can never be free." However, in 1857, after eight years of captivity, he was sent to the comparative freedom of Siberia. From there, in 1861, he succeeded in escaping to Japan, and thence through America to London. He had been imprisoned for his hostility to governments, but, strange to say, his sufferings had not had the intended effect of making him love those who inflicted them. From this time onward, he devoted himself to spreading the spirit of Anarchist revolt, without, however, having to suffer any further term of imprisonment. For some years he lived in Italy, where he founded in 1864 an " International Fraternity " or " Alliance of Socialist Revolutionaries." This contained men of many countries, but apparently no Germans. It devoted itself largely to combating Mazzini's nationalism. In 1867 he moved to Switzerland, where in the following year he helped to found the " International Alliance of So-

---
[1] Ibid. p. xxvi.

cialist Democracy," of which he drew up the program. This program gives a good succinct *résumé* of his opinons:—

The Alliance declares itself atheist; it desires the definitive and entire abolition of classes and the political equality and social equalization of individuals of both sexes. It desires that the earth, the instrument of labor, like all other capital, becoming the collective property of society as a whole, shall be no longer able to be utilized except by the workers, that is to say, by agricultural and industrial associations. It recognizes that all actually existing political and authoritarian States, reducing themselves more and more to the mere administrative functions of the public services in their respective countries, must disappear in the universal union of free associations, both agricultural and industrial.

The International Alliance of Socialist Democracy desired to become a branch of the International Working Men's Association, but was refused admission on the ground that branches must be local, and could not themselves be international. The Geneva group of the Alliance, however, was admitted later, in July, 1869.

The International Working Men's Association had been founded in London in 1864, and its statutes and program were drawn up by Marx. Bakunin at first did not expect it to prove a success and refused to join it. But it spread with remarkable rapidity in many countries and soon became a great power for the propagation of Socialist ideas. Originally it was by no means wholly Socialist, but in successive Congresses Marx won it over more and more to his views. At its third Congress, in Brussels in September, 1868, it became definitely Socialist. Meanwhile Bakunin, regretting his earlier abstention, had decided to join it, and he brought with him a considerable following in French-Switzerland, France, Spain and Italy. At the fourth Congress, held at Basle in September, 1869, two currents were strongly marked. The Germans and English followed Marx in his belief in the State as it was to become after the abolition of private property; they followed him also in his desire to found Labor Parties in the various countries, and to utilize the machinery of democracy for the election of representatives of Labor to Parliaments. On the other hand, the Latin nations in the main followed Bakunin in opposing the State and disbelieving in the machinery of representative government. The conflict between these two groups grew more and more bitter, and each accused the other of various offenses. The statement that Bakunin was a spy was repeated, but was withdrawn after investigation. Marx wrote in a confidential communication to his German friends that Bakunin was an agent of the Pan-Slavist party and received from them 25,000 francs a year. Meanwhile, Bakunin became for a time interested in the attempt to stir up an agrarian revolt in Russia, and this led him to neglect the contest in the International at a crucial moment. During the Franco-Prussian war Bakunin passionately took the side of France, especially after the fall of Napoleon III. He endeavored to rouse the people to revolutionary resistance like that of 1793, and became involved in an abortive attempt at revolt in Lyons. The French Government accused him of being a paid agent of Prussia, and it was with difficulty that he escaped to Switzerland. The dispute with Marx and his followers had become exacerbated by the national dispute. Bakunin, like Kropotkin after him, regarded the new power of Germany as the greatest menace to liberty in the world. He hated the Germans with a bitter hatred, partly, no doubt, on account of Bismarck, but probably still more on account of Marx. To this day, Anarchism has remained confined almost exclusively to the Latin countries, and has been associated with a hatred of Germany, growing out of the contests between Marx and Bakunin in the International.

The final suppression of Bakunin's faction occurred at the General Congress of the International at the Hague in 1872. The meeting-place was chosen by the General Council (in which Marx was unopposed), with a view—so Bakunin's friends contend—to making access impossible for Bakunin (on

BAKUNIN AND ANARCHISM 47

account of the hostility of the French and German governments) and difficult for his friends. Bakunin was expelled from the International as the result of a report accusing him *inter alia* of theft backed up by intimidation.

The orthodoxy of the International was saved, but at the cost of its vitality. From this time onward, it ceased to be itself a power, but both sections continued to work in their various groups, and the Socialist groups in particular grew rapidly. Ultimately a new International was formed (1889) which continued down to the outbreak of the present war. As to the future of International Socialism it would be rash to prophesy, though it would seem that the international idea has acquired sufficient strength to need again, after the war, some such means of expression as it found before in Socialist congresses.

By this time Bakunin's health was broken, and except for a few brief intervals, he lived in retirement until his death in 1876.

Bakunin's life, unlike Marx's, was a very stormy one. Every kind of rebellion against authority always aroused his sympathy, and in his support he never paid the slightest attention to personal risk. His influence, undoubtedly very great, arose chiefly through the influence of his personality upon important individuals. His writings differ from Marx's as much as his life does, and in a similar way. They are chaotic, largely aroused by some passing occasion, abstract and metaphysical, except when they deal with current politics. He does not come to close quarters with economic facts, but dwells usually in the regions of theory and metaphysics. When he descends from these regions, he is much more at the mercy of current international politics than Marx, much less imbued with the consequences of the belief that it is economic causes that are fundamental. He praised Marx for enunciating this doctrine,[1] but nevertheless continued to think in terms of nations. His longest work, "L'Empire Knouto-Germanique et la Révolution Sociale," is mainly concerned with the situation in France during the later stages of the Franco-Prussian War, and with the means of resisting German imperialism. Most of his writing was done in a hurry in the interval between two insurrections. There is something of Anarchism in his lack of literary order. His best-known work is a fragment entitled by its editors "God and the State."[2]

---

[1] "Marx, as a thinker, is on the right road. He has established as a principle that all the evolutions, political, religious, and juridical, in history are, not the causes, but the effects of economic evolutions. This is a great and fruitful thought, which he has not absolutely invented; it has been glimpsed, expressed in part, by many others besides him; but in any case to him belongs the honor of having solidly established it and of having enunciated it as the basis of his whole economic system. (1870; ib. ii. p. xiii.)

[2] This title is not Bakunin's, but was invented by Cafiero and Elisée Reclus, who edited it, not knowing that it was a fragment of what was intended to be the second version of "L'Empire Knouto-Germanique" (see ib. ii. p 283).

In this work he represents belief in God and belief in the State as the two great obstacles to human liberty. A typical passage will serve to illustrate its style.

> The State is not society, it is only an historical form of it, as brutal as it is abstract. It was born historically in all countries of the marriage of violence, rapine, pillage, in a word, war and conquest, with the gods successively created by the theological fantasy of nations. It has been from its origin, and it remains still at present, the divine sanction of brutal force and triumphant inequality.
>
> The State is authority; it is force; it is the ostentation and infatuation of force: it does not insinuate itself; it does not seek to convert. . . . Even when it commands what is good, it hinders and spoils it, just because it commands it, and because every command provokes and excites the legitimate revolts of liberty; and because the good, from the moment that it is commanded, becomes evil from the point of view of true morality, of human morality (doubtless not of divine), from the point of view of human respect and of liberty. Liberty, morality, and the human dignity of man consist precisely in this, that he does good, not because it is commanded, but because he conceives it, wills it and loves it.

We do not find in Bakunin's works a clear picture of the society at which he aimed, or any argument to prove that such a society could be stable. If we wish to understand Anarchism we must turn to his followers, and especially to Kropotkin—like him, a Russian aristocrat familiar with the prisons of Europe, and, like him, an Anarchist who, in spite of his internationalism, is imbued with a fiery hatred of the Germans.

Kropotkin has devoted much of his writing to technical questions of production. In " Fields, Factories and Workshops " and " The Conquest of Bread " he has set himself to prove that, if production were more scientific and better organized, a comparatively small amount of quite agreeable work would suffice to keep the whole population in comfort. Even assuming, as we probably must, that he somewhat exaggerates what is possible with our present scientific knowledge, it must nevertheless be conceded that his contentions contain a very large measure of truth. In attacking the subject of production he has shown that he knows what is the really crucial question. If civilization and progress are to be compatible with equality, it is necessary that equality should not involve long hours of painful toil for little more than the necessaries of life, since, where there is no leisure, art and science will die and all progress will become impossible. The objection which some feel to Socialism and Anarchism alike on this ground cannot be upheld in view of the possible productivity of labor.

The system at which Kropotkin aims, whether or

BAKUNIN AND ANARCHISM 51

not it be possible, is certainly one which demands a very great improvement in the methods of production above what is common at present. He desires to abolish wholly the system of wages, not only, as most Socialists do, in the sense that a man is to be paid rather for his willingness to work than for the actual work demanded of him, but in a more fundamental sense: there is to be no obligation to work, and all things are to be shared in equal proportions among the whole population. Kropotkin relies upon the possibility of making work pleasant: he holds that, in such a community as he foresees, practically everyone will prefer work to idleness, because work will not involve overwork or slavery, or that excessive specialization that industrialism has brought about, but will be merely a pleasant activity for certain hours of the day, giving a man an outlet for his spontaneous constructive impulses. There is to be no compulsion, no law, no government exercising force; there will still be acts of the community, but these are to spring from universal consent, not from any enforced submission of even the smallest minority. We shall examine in a later chapter how far such an ideal is realizable, but it cannot be denied that Kropotkin presents it with extraordinary persuasiveness and charm.

We should be doing more than justice to Anarchism if we did not say something of its darker side, the side which has brought it into conflict with the police and made it a word of terror to ordinary citizens. In its general doctrines there is nothing essentially involving violent methods or a virulent hatred of the rich, and many who adopt these general doctrines are personally gentle and temperamentally averse from violence. But the general tone of the Anarchist press and public is bitter to a degree that seems scarcely sane, and the appeal, especially in Latin countries, is rather to envy of the fortunate than to pity for the unfortunate. A vivid and readable, though not wholly reliable, account, from a hostile point of view, is given in a book called "Le Péril Anarchiste," by Félix Dubois,[1] which incidentally reproduces a number of cartoons from anarchist journals. The revolt against law naturally leads, except in those who are controlled by a real passion for humanity, to a relaxation of all the usually accepted moral rules, and to a bitter spirit of retaliatory cruelty out of which good can hardly come.

One of the most curious features of popular Anarchism is its martyrology, aping Christian forms, with the guillotine (in France) in place of the cross. Many who have suffered death at the hands of the authorities on account of acts of violence were no doubt genuine sufferers for their belief in a cause, but others, equally honored, are more questionable.

---

[1] Paris, 1894.

One of the most curious examples of this outlet for the repressed religious impulse is the cult of Ravachol, who was guillotined in 1892 on account of various dynamite outrages. His past was dubious, but he died defiantly; his last words were three lines from a well-known Anarchist song, the "Chant du Père Duchesne":—

> *Si tu veux être heureux,*
> *Nom de Dieu!*
> *Pends ton propriétaire.*

As was natural, the leading Anarchists took no part in the canonization of his memory; nevertheless it proceeded, with the most amazing extravagances.

It would be wholly unfair to judge Anarchist doctrine, or the views of its leading exponents, by such phenomena; but it remains a fact that Anarchism attracts to itself much that lies on the borderland of insanity and common crime.[1] This must be

---

[1] The attitude of all the better Anarchists is that expressed by L. S. Bevington in the words: "Of course we know that among those who call themselves Anarchists there are a minority of unbalanced enthusiasts who look upon every illegal and sensational act of violence as a matter for hysterical jubilation. Very useful to the police and the press, unsteady in intellect and of weak moral principle, they have repeatedly shown themselves accessible to venal considerations. They, and their violence, and their professed Anarchism are purchasable, and in the last resort they are welcome and efficient partisans of the bourgeoisie in its remorseless war against the deliverers of the people." His conclusion is a very wise one: "Let us leave indiscriminate killing and injuring to the Government—to its Statesmen, its Stockbrokers, its Officers, and its Law." ("Anarchism and Violence," pp. 9–10. Liberty Press, Chiswick, 1896.)

remembered in exculpation of the authorities and the thoughtless public, who often confound in a common detestation the parasites of the movement and the truly heroic and high-minded men who have elaborated its theories and sacrificed comfort and success to their propagation.

The terrorist campaign in which such men as Ravachol were active practically came to an end in 1894. After that time, under the influence of Pelloutier, the better sort of Anarchists found a less harmful outlet by advocating Revolutionary Syndicalism in the Trade Unions and *Bourses du Travail*.[1]

The *economic* organization of society, as conceived by Anarchist Communists, does not differ greatly from that which is sought by Socialists. Their difference from Socialists is in the matter of government: they demand that government shall require the consent of *all* the governed, and not only of a majority. It is undeniable that the rule of a majority may be almost as hostile to freedom as the rule of a minority: the divine right of majorities is a dogma as little possessed of absolute truth as any other. A strong democratic State may easily be led into oppression of its best citizens, namely, those whose independence of mind would make them a force for progress. Experience of democratic parliamentary government has shown that it falls very far

---

[1] See next Chapter.

short of what was expected of it by early Socialists, and the Anarchist revolt against it is not surprising. But in the form of pure Anarchism, this revolt has remained weak and sporadic. It is Syndicalism, and the movements to which Syndicalism has given rise, that have popularized the revolt against parliamentary government and purely political means of emancipating the wage-earner. But this movement must be dealt with in a separate chapter.

CHAPTER III

THE SYNDICALIST REVOLT

SYNDICALISM arose in France as a revolt against political Socialism, and in order to understand it we must trace in brief outline the positions attained by Socialist parties in the various countries.

After a severe setback, caused by the Franco-Prussian war, Socialism gradually revived, and in all the countries of Western Europe Socialist parties have increased their numerical strength almost continuously during the last forty years; but, as is invariably the case with a growing sect, the intensity of faith has diminished as the number of believers has increased.

In Germany the Socialist party became the strongest faction of the Reichstag, and, in spite of differences of opinion among its members, it preserved its formal unity with that instinct for military discipline which characterizes the German nation. In the Reichstag election of 1912 it polled a third of the total number of votes cast, and returned 110 members out of a total of 397. After the death of Bebel, the Revisionists, who received their first impulse from Bernstein, ovecame the more strict

THE SYNDICALIST REVOLT 57

Marxians, and the party became in effect merely one of advanced Radicalism. It is too soon to guess what will be the effect of the split between Majority and Minority Socialists which has occurred during the war. There is in Germany hardly a trace of Syndicalism; its characteristic doctrine, the preference of industrial to political action, has found scarcely any support.

In England Marx has never had many followers. Socialism there has been inspired in the main by the Fabians (founded in 1883), who threw over the advocacy of revolution, the Marxian doctrine of value, and the class-war. What remained was State Socialism and a doctrine of "permeation." Civil servants were to be permeated with the realization that Socialism would enormously increase their power. Trade Unions were to be permeated with the belief that the day for purely industrial action was past, and that they must look to government (inspired secretly by sympathetic civil servants) to bring about, bit by bit, such parts of the Socialist program as were not likely to rouse much hostility in the rich. The Independent Labor Party (formed in 1893) was largely inspired at first by the ideas of the Fabians, though retaining to the present day, and especially since the outbreak of the war, much more of the original Socialist ardor. It aimed always at co-operation with the industrial organizations of wage-earners, and, chiefly through its efforts, the Labor Party [1] was formed in 1900 out of a combination of the Trade Unions and the political Socialists. To this party, since 1909, all the important Unions have belonged, but in spite of the fact that its strength is derived from Trade Unions, it has stood always for political rather than industrial action. Its Socialism has been of a theoretical and academic order, and in practice, until the outbreak of war, the Labor members in Parliament (of whom 30 were elected in 1906 and 42 in December, 1910) might be reckoned almost as a part of the Liberal Party.

France, unlike England and Germany, was not content merely to repeat the old shibboleths with continually diminishing conviction. In France [2] a new movement, originally known as Revolutionary Syndicalism—and afterward simply as Syndicalism—kept alive the vigor of the original impulse, and remained true to the spirit of the older Socialists, while departing from the letter. Syndicalism, unlike Socialism and Anarchism, began from an existing organization and developed the ideas appropriate

---

[1] Of which the Independent Labor Party is only a section.
[2] And also in Italy. A good, short account of the Italian movement is given by A. Lanzillo, " Le Mouvement Ouvrier en Italie," Bibliothèque du Mouvement Prolétarien. See also Paul Louis, " Le Syndicalisme Européen," chap. vi. On the other hand Cole ("World of Labour," chap. vi) considers the strength of genuine Syndicalism in Italy to be small.

THE SYNDICALIST REVOLT

to it, whereas Socialism and Anarchism began with the ideas and only afterward developed the organizations which were their vehicle. In order to understand Syndicalism, we have first to describe Trade Union organization in France, and its political environment. The ideas of Syndicalism will then appear as the natural outcome of the political and economic situation. Hardly any of these ideas are new; almost all are derived from the Bakunist section of the old International.[1] The old International had considerable success in France before the Franco-Prussian War; indeed, in 1869, it is estimated to have had a French membership of a quarter of a million. What is practically the Syndicalist program was advocated by a French delegate to the Congress of the International at Bâle in that same year.[2]

The war of 1870 put an end for the time being to the Socialist Movement in France. Its revival was begun by Jules Guesde in 1877. Unlike the Ger-

---

[1] This is often recognized by Syndicalists themselves. See, *e.g.*, an article on "The Old International" in the *Syndicalist* of February, 1913, which, after giving an account of the struggle between Marx and Bakunin from the standpoint of a sympathizer with the latter, says: "Bakounin's ideas are now more alive than ever."

[2] See pp. 42–43, and 160 of "Syndicalism in France," Louis Levine, Ph.D. (Columbia University Studies in Political Science, vol. xlvi, No. 3.) This is a very objective and reliable account of the origin and progress of French Syndicalism. An admirable short discussion of its ideas and its present position will be found in Cole's "World of Labour" (G. Bell & Sons), especially chapters iii, iv, and xi.

man Socialists, the French have been split into many different factions. In the early eighties there was a split between the Parliamentary Socialists and the Communist Anarchists. The latter thought that the first act of the Social Revolution should be the destruction of the State, and would therefore have nothing to do with Parliamentary politics. The Anarchists, from 1883 onward, had success in Paris and the South. The Socialists contended that the State will disappear after the Socialist society has been firmly established. In 1882 the Socialists split between the followers of Guesde, who claimed to represent the revolutionary and scientific Socialism of Marx, and the followers of Paul Brousse, who were more opportunist and were also called *possibilists* and cared little for the theories of Marx. In 1890 there was a secession from the Broussists, who followed Allemane and absorbed the more revolutionary elements of the party and became leading spirits in some of the strongest syndicates. Another group was the Independent Socialists, among whom were Jaurès, Millerand and Viviani.[1]

The disputes between the various sections of Socialists caused difficulties in the Trade Unions and helped to bring about the resolution to keep politics out of the Unions. From this to Syndicalism was an easy step.

---

[1] See Levine, *op. cit.*, chap. ii.

THE SYNDICALIST REVOLT 61

Since the year 1905, as the result of a union between the *Parti Socialiste de France* (*Parti Ouvrier Socialiste Révolutionnaire Français* led by Guesde) and the *Parti Socialiste Français* (Jaurès), there have been only two groups of Socialists, the United Socialist Party and the Independents, who are intellectuals or not willing to be tied to a party. At the General Election of 1914 the former secured 102 members and the latter 30, out of a total of 590.

Tendencies toward a *rapprochement* between the various groups were seriously interfered with by an event which had considerable importance for the whole development of advanced political ideas in France, namely, the acceptance of office in the Waldeck-Rousseau Ministry by the Socialist Millerand in 1899. Millerand, as was to be expected, soon ceased to be a Socialist, and the opponents of political action pointed to his development as showing the vanity of political triumphs. Very many French politicians who have risen to power have begun their political career as Socialists, and have ended it not infrequently by employing the army to oppress strikers. Millerand's action was the most notable and dramatic among a number of others of a similar kind. Their cumulative effect has been to produce a certain cynicism in regard to politics among the more class-conscious of French wage-earners, and this state of mind greatly assisted the spread of Syndicalism.

Syndicalism stands essentially for the point of view of the producer as opposed to that of the consumer; it is concerned with reforming actual work, and the organization of industry, not *merely* with securing greater rewards for work. From this point of view its vigor and its distinctive character are derived. It aims at substituting industrial for political action, and at using Trade Union organization for purposes for which orthodox Socialism would look to Parliament. "Syndicalism" was originally only the French name for Trade Unionism, but the Trade Unionists of France became divided into two sections, the Reformist and the Revolutionary, of whom the latter only professed the ideas which we now associate with the term "Syndicalism." It is quite impossible to guess how far either the organization or the ideas of the Syndicalists will remain intact at the end of the war, and everything that we shall say is to be taken as applying only to the years before the war. It may be that French Syndicalism as a distinctive movement will be dead, but even in that case it will not have lost its importance, since it has given a new impulse and direction to the more vigorous part of the labor movement in all civilized countries, with the possible exception of Germany.

The organization upon which Syndicalism de

pended was the *Confédération Générale du Travail*, commonly known as the C. G. T., which was founded in 1895, but only achieved its final form in 1902. It has never been numerically very powerful, but has derived its influence from the fact that in moments of crisis many who were not members were willing to follow its guidance. Its membership in the year before the war is estimated by Mr. Cole at somewhat more than half a million. Trade Unions (*Syndicats*) were legalized by Waldeck-Rousseau in 1884, and the C. G. T., on its inauguration in 1895, was formed by the Federation of 700 *Syndicats*. Alongside of this organization there existed another, the *Fédération des Bourses du Travail*, formed in 1893. A *Bourse du Travail* is a local organization, not of any one trade, but of local labor in general, intended to serve as a Labor Exchange and to perform such functions for labor as Chambers of Commerce perform for the employer.[1] A *Syndicat* is in general a local organization of a single industry, and is thus a smaller unit than the *Bourse du Travail*.[2] Under the able leadership of Pelloutier, the *Fédération des Bourses* prospered more than the C. G. T., and at last, in 1902, coalesced with it. The result was an organization in which the local *Syndicat* was fed-

---

[1] Cole, ib., p. 65.
[2] "*Syndicat* in France still means a *local* union—there are at the present day only four national *syndicats*" (ib., p. 66).

erated twice over, once with the other *Syndicat* in its locality, forming together the local *Bourse du Travail*, and again with the *Syndicats* in the same industry in other places. "It was the purpose of the new organization to secure twice over the membership of every *syndicat*, to get it to join both its local *Bourse du Travail* and the Federation of its industry. The Statutes of the C. G. T. (I. 3) put this point plainly: 'No *Syndicat* will be able to form a part of the C. G. T. if it is not federated nationally and an adherent of a *Bourse du Travail* or a local or departmental Union of *Syndicats* grouping different associations.' Thus, M. Lagardelle explains, the two sections will correct each other's point of view: national federation of industries will prevent parochialism (*localisme*), and local organization will check the corporate or 'Trade Union' spirit. The workers will learn at once the solidarity of all workers in a locality and that of all workers in a trade, and, in learning this, they will learn at the same time the complete solidarity of the whole working-class."[1]

This organization was largely the work of Pellouties, who was Secretary of the *Fédération des Bourses* from 1894 until his death in 1901. He was an Anarchist Communist and impressed his ideas upon the *Fédération* and thence posthumously on the C. G. T. after its combination with the *Fédération des*

---

[1] Cole, ib. p. 69.

Bourses. He even carried his principles into the government of the Federation; the Committee had no chairman and votes very rarely took place. He stated that "the task of the revolution is to free mankind, not only from all authority, but also from every institution which has not for its essential purpose the development of production."

The C. G. T. allows much autonomy to each unit in the organization. Each *Syndicat* counts for one, whether it be large or small. There are not the friendly society activities which form so large a part of the work of English Unions. It gives no orders, but is purely advisory. It does not allow politics to be introduced into the Unions. This decision was originally based upon the fact that the divisions among Socialists disrupted the Unions, but it is now reinforced in the minds of an important section by the general Anarchist dislike of politics. The C. G. T. is essentially a fighting organization; in strikes, it is the nucleus to which the other workers rally.

There is a Reformist section in the C. G. T., but it is practically always in a minority, and the C. G. T. is, to all intents and purposes, the organ of revolutionary Syndicalism, which is simply the creed of its leaders.

The essential doctrine of Syndicalism is the class-war, to be conducted by industrial rather than political methods. The chief industrial methods advocated are the strike, the boycott, the label and sabotage.

The boycott, in various forms, and the label, showing that the work has been done under trade-union conditions, have played a considerable part in American labor struggles.

Sabotage is the practice of doing bad work, or spoiling machinery or work which has already been done, as a method of dealing with employers in a dispute when a strike appears for some reason undesirable or impossible. It has many forms, some clearly innocent, some open to grave objections. One form of sabotage which has been adopted by shop assistants is to tell customers the truth about the articles they are buying; this form, however it may damage the shopkeeper's business, is not easy to object to on moral grounds. A form which has been adopted on railways, particularly in Italian strikes, is that of obeying all rules literally and exactly, in such a way as to make the running of trains practically impossible. Another form is to do all the work with minute care, so that in the end it is better done, but the output is small. From these innocent forms there is a continual progression, until we come to such acts as all ordinary morality would consider criminal; for example, causing railway accidents. Advocates of sabotage justify it as part of war, but in its more violent forms (in which it is seldom defended) it is cruel and probably inexpedient, while even in its milder forms it must tend to encourage slovenly habits of work, which might easily persist under the new régime that the Syndicalists wish to introduce. At the same time, when capitalists express a moral horror of this method, it is worth while to observe that they themselves are the first to practice it when the occasion seems to them appropriate. If report speaks truly, an example of this on a very large scale has been seen during the Russian Revolution.

By far the most important of the Syndicalist methods is the strike. Ordinary strikes, for specific objects, are regarded as rehearsals, as a means of perfecting organization and promoting enthusiasm, but even when they are victorious so far as concerns the specific point in dispute, they are not regarded by Syndicalists as affording any ground for industrial peace. Syndicalists aim at using the strike, not to secure such improvements of detail as employers may grant, but to destroy the whole system of employer and employed and win the complete emancipation of the worker. For this purpose what is wanted is the General Strike, the complete cessation of work by a sufficient proportion of the wage-earners to secure the paralysis of capitalism. Sorel, who represents Syndicalism too much in the minds of the reading public, suggests that the General Strike is to be regarded as a myth, like the Second Coming in Christian doctrine. But this view by no means suits the active Syndicalists. If they were brought to believe that the General Strike is a mere myth, their energy would flag, and their whole outlook would become disillusioned. It is the actual, vivid belief in its possibility which inspires them. They are much criticised for this belief by the political Socialists. who consider that the battle is to be won by obtaining a Parliamentary majority. But Syndicalists have too little faith in the honesty of politicians to place any reliance on such a method or to believe in the value of any revolution which leaves the power of the State intact.

Syndicalist aims are somewhat less definite than Syndicalist methods. The intellectuals who endeavor to interpret them—not always very faithfully—represent them as a party of movement and change, following a Bergsonian *élan vital*, without needing any very clear prevision of the goal to which it is to take them. Nevertheless, the negative part, at any rate, of their objects is sufficiently clear.

They wish to destroy the State, which they regard as a capitalist institution, designed essentially to terrorize the workers. They refuse to believe that it would be any better under State Socialism. They desire to see each industry self-governing, but as to the means of adjusting the relations between

THE SYNDICALIST REVOLT 69

different industries, they are not very clear. They are anti-militarist because they are anti-State, and because French troops have often been employed against them in strikes; also because they are internationalists, who believe that the sole interest of the working man everywhere is to free himself from the tyranny of the capitalist. Their outlook on life is the very reverse of pacifist, but they oppose wars between States on the ground that these are not fought for objects that in any way concern the workers. Their anti-militarism, more than anything else, brought them into conflict with the authorities in the years preceding the war. But, as was to be expected, it did not survive the actual invasion of France.

The doctrines of Syndicalism may be illustrated by an article introducing it to English readers in the first number of " The Syndicalist Railwayman," September, 1911, from which the following is quoted:—

"All Syndicalism, Collectivism, Anarchism aims at abolishing the present economic status and existing private ownership of most things; but while Collectivism would substitute ownership by everybody, and Anarchism ownership by nobody, Syndicalism aims at ownership by Organized Labor. It is thus a purely Trade Union reading of the economic doctrine and the class war preached by Socialism. It vehemently repudiates Parliamentary action on which Collectivism relies; and it is, in this respect, much more closely allied to Anarchism, from which, indeed, it differs in practice only in being more limited in range of action." (*Times,* Aug. 25, 1911).

In truth, so thin is the partition between Syndicalism and Anarchism that the newer and less familiar " ism " has been shrewdly defined as " Organized Anarchy." It has been created by the Trade Unions of France; but it is obviously an international plant, whose roots have already found the soil of Britain most congenial to its growth and fructification.

Collectivist or Marxian Socialism would have us believe that it is distinctly a *Labor* Movement; but it is not so. Neither is Anarchism. The one is substantially *bourgeois;* the other *aristocratic,* plus an abundant output of book-learning, in either case. Syndicalism, on the contrary, is indubitably *laborist* in origin and aim, owing next to nothing to the " Classes," and, indeed, resolute to uproot them. The *Times* (Oct. 13, 1910), which almost single-handed in the British Press has kept creditably abreast of Continental Syndicalism, thus clearly set forth the significance of the General Strike:

"To understand what it means, we must remember that there is in France a powerful Labor Organization, which has for its open and avowed object a Revolution, in which not only the present order of Society, but the State itself, is to be swept away. This movement is called Syndicalism. It is not Socialism, but, on the contrary, radically opposed to Socialism, because the Syndicalists hold that the State is the great enemy and that the Socialists' ideal of State or Collectivist Ownership would make the lot of the Workers much worse than it is now under private employers. The means by which they hope to attain their end is the General Strike, an idea which was invented by a French workman about twenty years ago,[1] and was adopted by the French Labor Congress in 1894, after a furious battle with the Socialists, in which the latter were worsted. Since then the General Strike has been the avowed policy of the Syndicalists, whose organization is the Confédération Générale du Travail."

Or, to put it otherwise, the intelligent French worker has awakened, as he believes, to the fact that Society (Societas) and the State (Civitas) connote two separable spheres of human activity, between which there is no connection, necessary or desirable. Without the one, man, being a gregarious animal, cannot subsist: while without the other he would simply be in clover. The "statesman" whom office does not render positively nefarious is at best an expensive superfluity.

Syndicalists have had many violent encounters with the forces of government. In 1907 and 1908, protesting against bloodshed which had occurred in the suppression of strikes, the Committee of the C. G. T. issued manifestoes speaking of the Government as " a Government of assassins " and alluding to the Prime Minister as " Clemenceau the murderer." Similar events in the strike at Villeneuve St. Georges in 1908 led to the arrest of all the leading members

---

[1] In fact the General Strike was invented by a Londoner, William Benbow, an Owenite, in 1831.

of the Committee. In the railway strike of October, 1910, Monsieur Briand arrested the Strike Committee, mobilized the railway men and sent soldiers to replace strikers. As a result of these vigorous measures the strike was completely defeated, and after this the chief energy of the C. G. T. was directed against militarism and nationalism.

The attitude of Anarchism to the Syndicalist movement is sympathetic, with the reservation that such methods as the General Strike are not to be regarded as substitutes for the violent revolution which most Anarchists consider necessary. Their attitude in this matter was defined at the International Anarchist Congress held in Amsterdam in August, 1907. This Congress recommended " comrades of all countries to actively participate in autonomous movements of the working class, and to develop in Syndicalist organizations the ideas of revolt, individual initiative and solidarity, which are the essence of Anarchism." Comrades were to " propagate and support only those forms and manifestations of direct action which carry, in themselves, a revolutionary character and lead to the transformation of society." It was resolved that " the Anarchists think that the destruction of the capitalist and authoritary society can only be realized by armed insurrection and violent expropriation, and that the use of the more or less General Strike

THE SYNDICALIST REVOLT 73

and the Syndicalist movement must not make us forget the more direct means of struggle against the military force of government."

Syndicalists might retort that when the movement is strong enough to win by armed insurrection it will be abundantly strong enough to win by the General Strike. In Labor movements generally, success through violence can hardly be expected except in circumstances where success without violence is attainable. This argument alone, even if there were no other, would be a very powerful reason against the methods advocated by the Anarchist Congress.

Syndicalism stands for what is known as industrial unionism as opposed to craft unionism. In this respect, as also in the preference of industrial to political methods, it is part of a movement which has spread far beyond France. The distinction between industrial and craft unionism is much dwelt on by Mr. Cole. Craft unionism " unites in a single association those workers who are engaged on a single industrial process, or on processes so nearly akin that any one can do another's work." But " organization may follow the lines, not of the work done, but of the actual structure of industry. All workers working at producing a particular kind of commodity may be organized in a single Union. . . . The basis of organization would be neither the craft to which a man belonged nor the employer under whom he worked, but the service on which he was engaged. This is Industrial Unionism properly so called.[1]

Industrial unionism is a product of America, and from America it has to some extent spread to Great Britain. It is the natural form of fighting organization when the union is regarded as the means of carrying on the class war with a view, not to obtaining this or that minor amelioration, but to a radical revolution in the economic system. This is the point of view adopted by the "Industrial Workers of the World," commonly known as the I. W. W. This organization more or less corresponds in America to what the C. G. T. was in France before the war. The differences between the two are those due to the different economic circumstances of the two countries, but their spirit is closely analogous. The I. W. W. is not united as to the ultimate form which it wishes society to take. There are Socialists, Anarchists and Syndicalists among its members. But it is clear on the immediate practical issue, that the class war is the fundamental reality in the present relations of labor and capital, and that it is by industrial action, especially by the strike, that emancipation must be sought. The I. W. W., like the C. G. T., is not nearly so strong numerically as it is supposed to be by those who fear it. Its influence

---

[1] "World of Labour," pp. 212, 213.

is based, not upon its numbers, but upon its power of enlisting the sympathies of the workers in moments of crisis.

The labor movement in America has been characterized on both sides by very great violence. Indeed, the Secretary of the C. G. T., Monsieur Jouhaux, recognizes that the C. G. T. is mild in comparison with the I. W. W. "The I. W. W.," he says, "preach a policy of militant action, very necessary in parts of America, which would not do in France."[1] A very interesting account of it, from the point of view of an author who is neither wholly on the side of labor nor wholly on the side of the capitalist, but disinterestedly anxious to find some solution of the social question short of violence and revolution, is the work of Mr. John Graham Brooks, called "American Syndicalism: the I. W. W." (Macmillan, 1913). American labor conditions are very different from those of Europe. In the first place, the power of the trusts is enormous; the concentration of capital has in this respect proceeded more nearly on Marxian lines in America than anywhere else. In the second place, the great influx of foreign labor makes the whole problem quite different from any that arises in Europe. The older skilled workers, largely American born, have long been organized in the American

---

[1] Quoted in Cole, ib. p. 128.

Federation of Labor under Mr. Gompers. These represent an aristocracy of labor. They tend to work with the employers against the great mass of unskilled immigrants, and they cannot be regarded as forming part of anything that could be truly called a labor movement. "There are," says Mr. Cole, "now in America two working classes, with different standards of life, and both are at present almost impotent in the face of the employers. Nor is it possible for these two classes to unite or to put forward any demands. . . . The American Federation of Labor and the Industrial Workers of the World represent two different principles of combination; but they also represent two different classes of labor."[1] The I. W. W. stands for industrial unionism, whereas the American Federation of Labor stands for craft unionism. The I. W. W. were formed in 1905 by a union of organizations, chief among which was the Western Federation of Miners, which dated from 1892. They suffered a split by the loss of the followers of Deleon, who was the leader of the "Socialist Labor Party" and advocated a "Don't vote" policy, while reprobating violent methods. The headquarters of the party which he formed are at Detroit, and those of the main body are at Chicago. The I. W. W., though it has a less

---

[1] Ib., p. 135.

definite philosophy than French Syndicalism, is quite equally determined to destroy the capitalist system. As its secretary has said: " There is but one bargain the I. W. W. will make with the employing class— *complete surrender of all control of industry to the organized workers.*"[1] Mr. Haywood, of the Western Federation of Miners, is an out-and-out follower of Marx so far as concerns the class war and the doctrine of surplus value. But, like all who are in this movement, he attaches more importance to industrial as against political action than do the European followers of Marx. This is no doubt partly explicable by the special circumstances of America, where the recent immigrants are apt to be voteless. The fourth convention of the I. W. W. revised a preamble giving the general principles underlying its action. " The working class and the employing class," they say, " have nothing in common. There can be no peace so long as hunger and want are found among millions of the working people and the few, who make up the employing class, have all the good things of life. Between these two classes, a struggle must go on until the workers of the world organize as a class, take possession of the earth and the machinery of production, and abolish the wage system. . . . Instead of the conservative motto,

---

[1] Brooks, *op. cit.*, p. 79.

'A fair day's wages for a fair day's work,' we must inscribe on our banner the revolutionary watchword, 'Abolition of the wage system.' " [1]

Numerous strikes have been conducted or encouraged by the I. W. W. and the Western Federation of Miners. These strikes illustrate the class-war in a more bitter and extreme form than is to be found in any other part of the world. Both sides are always ready to resort to violence. The employers have armies of their own and are able to call upon the Militia and even, in a crisis, upon the United States Army. What French Syndicalists say about the State as a capitalist institution is peculiarly true in America. In consequence of the scandals thus arising, the Federal Government appointed a Commission on Industrial Relations, whose Report, issued in 1915, reveals a state of affairs such as it would be difficult to imagine in Great Britain. The report states that " the greatest disorders and most of the outbreaks of violence in connection with industrial disputes arise from the violation of what are considered to be fundamental rights, and from the perversion or subversion of governmental institutions " (p. 146). It mentions, among such perversions, the subservience of the judiciary to the mili-

---

[1] Brooks, *op. cit.*, pp. 86-87.

THE SYNDICALIST REVOLT

tary authorities,[1] the fact that during a labor dispute the life and liberty of every man within the State would seem to be at the mercy of the Governor (p. 72), and the use of State troops in policing strikes (p. 298). At Ludlow (Colorado) in 1914 (April 20) a battle of the militia and the miners took place, in which, as the result of the fire of the militia, a number of women and children were burned to death.[2] Many other instances of pitched battles could be given, but enough has been said to show the peculiar character of labor disputes in the United States. It may, I fear, be presumed that this character will remain so long as a very large proportion of labor consists of recent immigrants. When these difficulties pass away, as they must sooner or later, labor will more and more find its place in the community, and will tend to feel and inspire less of the bitter hostility which renders the more extreme forms of class war possible. When

---

[1] "Although uniformly held that the writ of *habeas corpus* can only be suspended by the legislature, in these labor disturbances the executive has in fact suspended or disregarded the writ. . . . In cases arising from labor agitations, the judiciary has uniformly upheld the power exercised by the military, and in no case has there been any protest against the use of such power or any attempt to curtail it, except in Montana, where the conviction of a civilian by military commission was annulled" ("Final Report of the Commission on Industrial Relations" (1915) appointed by the United States Congress," p. 58).

[2] *Literary Digest*, May 2 and May 16, 1914.

that time comes, the labor movement in America will probably begin to take on forms similar to those of Europe.

Meanwhile, though the forms are different, the aims are very similar, and industrial unionism, spreading from America, has had a considerable influence in Great Britain—an influence naturally reinforced by that of French Syndicalism. It is clear, I think, that the adoption of industrial rather than craft unionism is absolutely necessary if Trade Unionism is to succeed in playing that part in altering the economic structure of society which its advocates claim for it rather than for the political parties. Industrial unionism organizes men, as craft unionism does not, in accordance with the enemy whom they have to fight. English unionism is still very far removed from the industrial form, though certain industries, especially the railway men, have gone very far in this direction, and it is notable that the railway men are peculiarly sympathetic to Syndicalism and industrial unionism.

Pure Syndicalism, however, is not very likely to achieve wide popularity in Great Britain. Its spirit is too revolutionary and anarchistic for our temperament. It is in the modified form of Guild Socialism that the ideas derived from the C. G. T. and the I. W.

W. are tending to bear fruit.[1] This movement is as yet in its infancy and has no great hold upon the rank and file, but it is being ably advocated by a group of young men, and is rapidly gaining ground among those who will form Labor opinion in years to come. The power of the State has been so much increased during the war that those who naturally dislike things as they are, find it more and more difficult to believe that State omnipotence can be the road to the millennium. Guild Socialists aim at autonomy in

---

[1] The ideas of Guild Socialism were first set forth in "National Guilds," edited by A. R. Orage (Bell & Sons, 1914), and in Cole's "World of Labour" (Bell & Sons), first published in 1913. Cole's "Self-Government in Industry" (Bell & Sons, 1917) and Rickett & Bechhofer's "The Meaning of National Guilds" (Palmer & Hayward, 1918) should also be read, as well as various pamphlets published by the National Guilds League. The attitude of the Syndicalists to Guild Socialism is far from sympathetic. An article in "The Syndicalist" for February, 1914, speaks of it in the following terms: "Middle-class of the middle-class, with all the shortcomings (we had almost said 'stupidities') of the middle-classes writ large across it, 'Guild Socialism' stands forth as the latest lucubration of the middle-class mind. It is a 'cool steal' of the leading ideas of Syndicalism and a deliberate perversion of them. . . . We do protest against the 'State' idea . . . in Guild Socialism. Middle-class people, even when they become Socialists, cannot get rid of the idea that the working-class is their 'inferior'; that the workers need to be 'educated,' drilled, disciplined, and generally nursed for a very long time before they will be able to walk by themselves. The very reverse is actually the truth. . . . It is just the plain truth when we say that the ordinary wage-worker, of average intelligence, is better capable of taking care of himself than the half-educated middle-class man who wants to advise him. He knows how to make the wheels of the world go round."

industry, with consequent curtailment, but not abolition, of the power of the State. The system which they advocate is, I believe, the best hitherto proposed, and the one most likely to secure liberty without the constant appeals to violence which are to be feared under a purely Anarchist *régime*.

The first pamphlet of the "National Guilds League" sets forth their main principles. In industry each factory is to be free to control its own methods of production by means of elected managers. The different factories in a given industry are to be federated into a National Guild which will deal with marketing and the general interests of the industry as a whole. "The State would own the means of production as trustee for the community; the Guilds would manage them, also as trustees for the community, and would pay to the State a single tax or rent. Any Guild that chose to set its own interests above those of the community would be violating its trust, and would have to bow to the judgment of a tribunal equally representing the whole body of producers and the whole body of consumers. This Joint Committee would be the ultimate sovereign body, the ultimate appeal court of industry. It would fix not only Guild taxation, but also standard prices, and both taxation and prices would be periodically readjusted by it." Each Guild will be

THE SYNDICALIST REVOLT

entirely free to apportion what it receives among its members as it chooses, its members being all those who work in the industry which it covers. "The distribution of this collective Guild income among the members seems to be a matter for each Guild to decide for itself. Whether the Guilds would, sooner or later, adopt the principle of equal payment for every member, is open to discussion." Guild Socialism accepts from Syndicalism the view that liberty is not to be secured by making the State the employer: "The State and the Municipality as employers have turned out not to differ essentially from the private capitalist." Guild Socialists regard the State as consisting of the community in their capacity as consumers, while the Guilds will represent them in their capacity as producers; thus Parliament and the Guild Congress will be two co-equal powers representing consumers and producers respectively. Above both will be the joint Committee of Parliament and the Guild Congress for deciding matters involving the interests of consumers and producers alike. The view of the Guild Socialists is that State Socialism takes account of men only as consumers, while Syndicalism takes account of them only as producers. "The problem," say the Guild Socialists, "is to reconcile the two points of view. That is what advocates of National Guilds set out to do. The Syndicalist has claimed everything for the industrial organizations of producers, the Collectivist everything for the territorial or political organizations of consumers. Both are open to the same criticism; you cannot reconcile two points of view merely by denying one of them."[1] But although Guild Socialism represents an attempt at readjustment between two equally legitimate points of view, its impulse and force are derived from what it has taken over from Syndicalism. Like Syndicalism; it desires not primarily to make work better paid, but to secure this result along with others by making it in itself more interesting and more democratic in organization.

Capitalism has made of work a purely commercial activity, a soulless and a joyless thing. But substitute the national service of the Guilds for the profiteering of the few; substitute responsible labor for a saleable commodity; substitute self-government and decentralization for the bureaucracy and demoralizing hugeness of the modern State and the modern joint stock company; and then it may be just once more to speak of a " joy in labor," and once more to hope that men may be proud of quality and not only of quantity in their work. There is a cant of the Middle Ages, and a cant of "joy in labor," but it were better, perhaps, to risk that cant than to reconcile ourselves forever to the philosophy of Capitalism and of Collectivism, which declares that work is a necessary evil never to be made pleasant, and that

---

[1] The above quotations are all from the first pamphlet of the National Guilds League, " National Guilds, an Appeal to Trade Unionists."

the workers' only hope is a leisure which shall be longer, richer, and well adorned with municipal amenities.[1]

Whatever may be thought of the practicability of Syndicalism, there is no doubt that the ideas which it has put into the world have done a great deal to revive the labor movement and to recall it to certain things of fundamental importance which it had been in danger of forgetting. Syndicalists consider man as producer rather than consumer. They are more concerned to procure freedom in work than to increase material well-being. They have revived the quest for liberty, which was growing somewhat dimmed under the *régime* of Parliamentary Socialism, and they have reminded men that what our modern society needs is not a little tinkering here and there, nor the kind of minor readjustments to which the existing holders of power may readily consent, but a fundamental reconstruction, a sweeping away of all the sources of oppression, a liberation of men's constructive energies, and a wholly new way of conceiving and regulating production and economic relations. This merit is so great that, in view of it, all minor defects become insignificant, and this merit Syndicalism will continue to possess even if, as a definite movement, it should be found to have passed away with the war.

---

[1] "The Guild Idea," No. 2 of the Pamphlets of the National Guilds League, p. 17.

PART II

PROBLEMS OF THE FUTURE

CHAPTER IV

WORK AND PAY

THE man who seeks to create a better order of society has two resistances to contend with: one that of Nature, the other that of his fellow-men. Broadly speaking, it is science that deals with the resistance of Nature, while politics and social organization are the methods of overcoming the resistance of men.

The ultimate fact in economics is that Nature only yields commodities as the result of labor. The necessity of *some* labor for the satisfaction of our wants is not imposed by political systems or by the exploitation of the working classes; it is due to physical laws, which the reformer, like everyone else, must admit and study. Before any optimistic economic project can be accepted as feasible, we must examine whether the physical conditions of production impose an unalterable veto, or whether they are capable of being sufficiently modified by science and organization. Two connected doctrines must be considered in examining this question: First, Malthus' doctrine of population; and second, the vaguer, but very prevalent, view that any surplus above the bare necessaries of life can only be produced if most men work long hours at monotonous or painful tasks, leaving little leisure for a civilized existence or rational enjoyment. I do not believe that either of these obstacles to optimism will survive a close scrutiny. The possibility of technical improvement in the methods of production is, I believe, so great that, at any rate for centuries to come, there will be no inevitable barrier to progress in the general well-being by the simultaneous increase of commodities and diminution of hours of labor.

This subject has been specially studied by Kropotkin, who, whatever may be thought of his general theories of politics, is remarkably instructive, concrete and convincing in all that he says about the possibilities of agriculture. Socialists and Anarchists in the main are products of industrial life, and few among them have any practical knowledge on the subject of food production. But Kropotkin is an exception. His two books, " The Conquest of Bread " and " Fields, Factories and Workshops," are very full of detailed information, and, even making great allowances for an optimistic bias, I do not think it can be denied that they demonstrate possibilities in which few of us would otherwise have believed.

Malthus contended, in effect, that population

always tends to increase up to the limit of subsistence, that the production of food becomes more expensive as its amount is increased, and that therefore, apart from short exceptional periods when new discoveries produce temporary alleviations, the bulk of mankind must always be at the lowest level consistent with survival and reproduction. As applied to the civilized races of the world, this doctrine is becoming untrue through the rapid decline in the birth-rate; but, apart from this decline, there are many other reasons why the doctrine cannot be accepted, at any rate as regards the near future. The century which elapsed after Malthus wrote, saw a very great increase in the standard of comfort throughout the wage-earning classes, and, owing to the enormous increase in the productivity of labor, a far greater rise in the standard of comfort could have been effected if a more just system of distribution had been introduced. In former times, when one man's labor produced not very much more than was needed for one man's subsistence, it was impossible either greatly to reduce the normal hours of labor, or greatly to increase the proportion of the population who enjoyed more than the bare necessaries of life. But this state of affairs has been overcome by modern methods of production. At the present moment, not only do many people enjoy a comfortable income derived from rent or interest, but about half the population of most of the civilized countries in the world is engaged, not in the production of commodities, but in fighting or in manufacturing munitions of war. In a time of peace the whole of this half might be kept in idleness without making the other half poorer than they would have been if the war had continued, and if, instead of being idle, they were productively employed, the whole of what they would produce would be a divisible surplus over and above present wages. The present productivity of labor in Great Britain would suffice to produce an income of about £1 per day for each family, even without any of those improvements in methods which are obviously immediately possible.

But, it will be said, as population increases, the price of food must ultimately increase also as the sources of supply in Canada, the Argentine, Australia and elsewhere are more and more used up. There must come a time, so pessimists will urge, when food becomes so dear that the ordinary wage-earner will have little surplus for expenditure upon other things. It may be admitted that this would be true in some very distant future if the population were to continue to increase without limit. If the whole surface of the world were as densely populated as London is now, it would, no doubt, require almost the whole labor of the population to produce the necessary food from the few spaces remaining for agriculture. But there is no reason to suppose that the population will continue to increase indefinitely, and in any case the prospect is so remote that it may be ignored in all practical considerations.

Returning from these dim speculations to the facts set forth by Kropotkin, we find it proved in his writings that, by methods of intensive cultivation, which are already in actual operation, the amount of food produced on a given area can be increased far beyond anything that most uninformed persons suppose possible. Speaking of the market-gardeners in Great Britain, in the neighborhood of Paris, and in other places, he says:—

> They have created a totally new agriculture. They smile when we boast about the rotation system having permitted us to take from the field one crop every year, or four crops each three years, because their ambition is to have six and nine crops from the very same plot of land during the twelve months. They do not understand our talk about good and bad soils, because they make the soil themselves, and make it in such quantities as to be compelled yearly to sell some of it; otherwise it would raise up the level of their gardens by half an inch every year. They aim at cropping, not five or six tons of grass on the acre, as we do, but from 50 to 100 tons of various vegetables on the same space; not £5 worth of hay, but £100 worth of vegetables, of the plainest description, cabbage and carrots.[1]

---
[1] Kropotkin, "Fields, Factories, and Workshops," p. 74.

WORK AND PAY

As regards cattle, he mentions that Mr. Champion at Whitby grows on each acre the food of two or three head of cattle, whereas under ordinary high farming it takes two or three acres to keep each head of cattle in Great Britain. Even more astonishing are the achievements of the Culture Maraîchères round Paris. It is impossible to summarize these achievements, but we may note the general conclusion:—

There are now practical Maraîchers who venture to maintain that if all the food, animal and vegetable, necessary for the 3,500,000 inhabitants of the Departments of Seine and Seine-et-Oise had to be grown on their own territory (3250 square miles), it could be grown without resorting to any other methods of culture than those already in use—methods already tested on a large scale and proved successful.[1]

It must be remembered that these two departments include the whole population of Paris.

Kropotkin proceeds to point out methods by which the same result could be achieved without long hours of labor. Indeed, he contends that the great bulk of agricultural work could be carried on by people whose main occupations are sedentary, and with only such a number of hours as would serve to keep them in health and produce a pleasant diversification. He protests against the theory of exces-

[1] Ib. p. 81.

sive division of labor. What he wants is *integration*, "a society where each individual is a producer of both manual and intellectual work; where each able-bodied human being is a worker, and where each worker works both in the field and in the industrial workshop."[1]

These views as to production have no essential connection with Kropotkin's advocacy of Anarchism. They would be equally possible under State Socialism, and under certain circumstances they might even be carried out in a capitalistic *régime*. They are important for our present purpose, not from any argument which they afford in favor of one economic system as against another, but from the fact that they remove the veto upon our hopes which might otherwise result from a doubt as to the productive capacity of labor. I have dwelt upon agriculture rather than industry, since it is in regard to agriculture that the difficulties are chiefly supposed to arise. Broadly speaking, industrial production tends to be cheaper when it is carried on on a large scale, and therefore there is no reason in industry why an increase in the demand should lead to an increased cost of supply.

Passing now from the purely technical and material side of the problem of production, we come

---

[1] Kropotkin, "Field, Factories, and Workshops," p. 6.

to the human factor, the motives leading men to work, the possibilities of efficient organization of production, and the connection of production with distribution. Defenders of the existing system maintain that efficient work would be impossible without the economic stimulus, and that if the wage system were abolished men would cease to do enough work to keep the community in tolerable comfort. Through the alleged necessity of the economic motive, the problems of production and distribution become intertwined. The desire for a more just distribution of the world's goods is the main inspiration of most Socialism and Anarchism. We must, therefore, consider whether the system of distribution which they propose would be likely to lead to a diminished production.

There is a fundamental difference between Socialism and Anarchism as regards the question of distribution. Socialism, at any rate in most of its forms, would retain payment for work done or for willingness to work, and, except in the case of persons incapacitated by age or infirmity, would make willingness to work a condition of subsistence, or at any rate of subsistence above a certain very low minimum. Anarchism, on the other hand, aims at granting to everyone, without any conditions whatever, just as much of all ordinary commodities as he or she may care to consume, while the rarer commodities, of which the supply cannot easily be indefinitely increased, would be rationed and divided equally among the population. Thus Anarchism would not impose any *obligation* of work, though Anarchists believe that the necessary work could be made sufficiently agreeable for the vast majority of the population to undertake it voluntarily. Socialists, on the other hand, would exact work. Some of them would make the incomes of all workers equal, while others would retain higher pay for the work which is considered more valuable. All these different systems are compatible with the common ownership of land and capital, though they differ greatly as regards the kind of society which they would produce.

Socialism with inequality of income would not differ greatly as regards the economic stimulus to work from the society in which we live. Such differences as it would entail would undoubtedly be to the good from our present point of view. Under the existing system many people enjoy idleness and affluence through the mere accident of inheriting land or capital. Many others, through their activities in industry or finance, enjoy an income which is certainly very far in excess of anything to which their social utility entitles them. On the other hand, it often happens that inventors and discoverers, whose work has the very greatest social utility, are robbed

WORK AND PAY

of their reward either by capitalists or by the failure of the public to appreciate their work until too late. The better paid work is only open to those who have been able to afford an expensive training, and these men are selected in the main not by merit but by luck. The wage-earner is not paid for his willingness to work, but only for his utility to the employer. Consequently, he may be plunged into destitution by causes over which he has no control. Such destitution is a constant fear, and when it occurs it produces undeserved suffering, and often deterioration in the social value of the sufferer. These are a few among the evils of our existing system from the standpoint of production. All these evils we might expect to see remedied under any system of Socialism.

There are two questions which need to be considered when we are discussing how far work requires the economic motive. The first question is: Must society give higher pay for the more skilled or socially more valuable work, if such work is to be done in sufficient quantities ? The second question is: Could work be made so attractive that enough of it would be done even if idlers received just as much of the produce of work? The first of these questions concerns the division between two schools of Socialists: the more moderate Socialists sometimes concede that even under Socialism it would be well to retain unequal pay for different kinds of work, while the more thoroughgoing Socialists advocate equal incomes for all workers. The second question, on the other hand, forms a division between Socialists and Anarchists; the latter would not deprive a man of commodities if he did not work, while the former in general would.

Our second question is so much more fundamental than our first that it must be discussed at once, and in the course of this discussion what needs to be said on our first question will find its place naturally.

Wages or Free Sharing?—"Abolition of the wages system" is one of the watchwords common to Anarchists and advanced Socialists. But in its most natural sense it is a watchword to which only the Anarchists have a right. In the Anarchist conception of society all the commoner commodities will be available to everyone without stint, in the kind of way in which water is available at present.[1] Advo-

---

[1] "Notwithstanding the egotistic turn given to the public mind by the merchant-production of our century, the Communist tendency is continually reasserting itself and trying to make its way into public life. The penny bridge disappears before the public bridge; and the turnpike road before the free road. The same spirit pervades thousands of other institutions. Museums, free libraries, and free public schools; parks and pleasure grounds; paved and lighted streets, free for everybody's use; water supplied to private dwellings, with a growing tendency towards disregarding the exact amount of it used by the individual; tramways and railways which have already begun to introduce the season ticket or the uniform tax, and will surely go much further on this line when they are no longer private property: all these are tokens showing in what direction further progress is to be expected."—Kropotkin, "Anarchist Communism."

cates of this system point out that it applies already to many things which formerly had to be paid for, *e.g.*, roads and bridges. They point out that it might very easily be extended to trams and local trains. They proceed to argue—as Kropotkin does by means of his proofs that the soil might be made indefinitely more productive—that all the commoner kinds of food could be given away to all who demanded them, since it would be easy to produce them in quantities adequate to any possible demand. If this system were extended to all the necessaries of life, everyone's bare livelihood would be secured, quite regardless of the way in which he might choose to spend his time. As for commodities which cannot be produced in indefinite quantities, such as luxuries and delicacies, they also, according to the Anarchists, are to be distributed without payment, but on a system of rations, the amount available being divided equally among the population. No doubt, though this is not said, something like a price will have to be put upon these luxuries, so that a man may be free to choose how he will take his share: one man will prefer good wine, another the finest Havana cigars, another pictures or beautiful furniture. Presumably, every man will be allowed to take such luxuries as are his due in whatever form he prefers, the relative prices being fixed so as to equalize the demand. In such a world as this, the economic stimulus to production will have wholly disappeared, and if work is to continue it must be from other motives.[1]

Is such a system possible? First, is it technically possible to provide the necessaries of life in such large quantities as would be needed if every man and woman could take as much of them from the public stores as he or she might desire?

The idea of purchase and payment is so familiar that the proposal to do away with it must be thought at first fantastic. Yet I do not believe it is nearly so fantastic as it seems. Even if we could all have bread for nothing, we should not want more than a quite limited amount. As things are, the cost of bread to the rich is so small a proportion of their income as to afford practically no check upon their consumption; yet the amount of bread that they consume could easily be supplied to the whole population by improved methods of agriculture (I am not speaking of war-time). The amount of food that people desire has natural limits, and the waste that would be incurred would probably not be very great. As the Anarchists point out, people at present enjoy an unlimited water supply but very few leave the taps running when they are not using them. And

---

[1] An able discussion of this question, as of various others, from the standpoint of reasoned and temperate opposition to Anarchism, will be found in Alfred Naquet's "L'Anarchie et le Collectivisme," Paris, 1904.

one may assume that public opinion would be opposed to excessive waste. We may lay it down, I think, that the principle of unlimited supply could be adopted in regard to all commodities for which the demand has limits that fall short of what can be easily produced. And this would be the case, if production were efficiently organized, with the necessaries of life, including not only commodities, but also such things as education. Even if all education were free up to the highest, young people, unless they were radically transformed by the Anarchist *régime*, would not want more than a certain amount of it. And the same applies to plain foods, plain clothes, and the rest of the things that supply our elementary needs.

I think we may conclude that there is no technical impossibility in the Anarchist plan of free sharing.

But would the necessary work be done if the individual were assured of the general standard of comfort even though he did no work?

Most people will answer this question unhesitatingly in the negative. Those employers in particular who are in the habit of denouncing their employes as a set of lazy, drunken louts, will feel quite certain that no work could be got out of them except under threat of dismissal and consequent starvation. But is this as certain as people are inclined to suppose at first sight? If work were to remain what most work is now, no doubt it would be very hard to induce people to undertake it except from fear of destitution. But there is no reason why work should remain the dreary drudgery in horrible conditions that most of it is now.[1] If men had to be tempted to work instead of driven to it, the obvious interest of the community would be to make work pleasant. So long as work is not made on the whole pleasant, it cannot be said that anything like a good state of society has been reached. Is the painfulness of work unavoidable?

At present, the better paid work, that of the business and professional classes, is for the most part enjoyable. I do not mean that every separate

---

[1] "Overwork is repulsive to human nature—not work. Overwork for supplying the few with luxury—not work for the well-being of all. Work, labor, is a physiological necessity, a necessity of spending accumulated bodily energy, a necessity which is health and life itself. If so many branches of useful work are so reluctantly done now, it is merely because they mean overwork, or they are improperly organized. But we know—old Franklin knew it—that four hours of useful work every day would be more than sufficient for supplying everybody with the comfort of a moderately well-to-do middle-class house, if we all gave ourselves to productive work, and if we did not waste our productive powers as we do waste them now. As to the childish question, repeated for fifty years: 'Who would do disagreeable work?' frankly I regret that none of our *savants* has ever been brought to do it, be it for only one day in his life. If there is still work which is really disagreeable in itself, it is only because our scientific men have never cared to consider the means of rendering it less so: they have always known that there were plenty of starving men who would do it for a few pence a day." Kropotkin, "'Anarchist Communism."

moment is agreeable, but that the life of a man who has work of this sort is on the whole happier than that of a man who enjoys an equal income without doing any work. A certain amount of effort, and something in the nature of a continuous career, are necessary to vigorous men if they are to preserve their mental health and their zest for life. A considerable amount of work is done without pay. People who take a rosy view of human nature might have supposed that the duties of a magistrate would be among disagreeable trades, like cleaning sewers; but a cynic might contend that the pleasures of vindictiveness and moral superiority are so great that there is no difficulty in finding well-to-do elderly gentlemen who are willing, without pay, to send helpless wretches to the torture of prison. And apart from enjoyment of the work itself, desire for the good opinion of neighbors and for the feeling of effectiveness is quite sufficient to keep many men active.

But, it will be said, the sort of work that a man would voluntarily choose must always be exceptional: the great bulk of necessary work can never be anything but painful. Who would choose, if an easy life were otherwise open to him, to be a coal-miner, or a stoker on an Atlantic liner? I think it must be conceded that much necessary work must always remain disagreeable or at least painfully monotonous, and that special privileges will have to be accorded to those who undertake it, if the Anarchist system is ever to be made workable. It is true that the introduction of such special privileges would somewhat mar the rounded logic of Anarchism, but it need not, I think, make any really vital breach in its system. Much of the work that needs doing could be rendered agreeable, if thought and care were given to this object. Even now it is often only long hours that make work irksome. If the normal hours of work were reduced to, say, four, as they could be by better organization and more scientific methods, a very great deal of work which is now felt as a burden would quite cease to be so. If, as Kropotkin suggests, agricultural work, instead of being the lifelong drudgery of an ignorant laborer living very near the verge of abject poverty, were the occasional occupation of men and women normally employed in industry or brain-work; if, instead of being conducted by ancient traditional methods, without any possibility of intelligent participation by the wage-earner, it were alive with the search for new methods and new inventions, filled with the spirit of freedom, and inviting the mental as well as the physical co-operation of those who do the work, it might become a joy instead of a weariness, and a source of health and life to those engaged in it.

What is true of agriculture is said by Anarchists to be equally true of industry. They maintain that if the great economic organizations which are now managed by capitalists, without consideration for the lives of the wage-earners beyond what Trade Unions are able to exact, were turned gradually into self-governing communities, in which the producers could decide all questions of methods, conditions, hours of work, and so forth, there would be an almost boundless change for the better: grime and noise might be nearly eliminated, the hideousness of industrial regions might be turned into beauty, the interest in the scientific aspects of production might become diffused among all producers with any native intelligence, and something of the artist's joy in creation might inspire the whole of the work. All this, which is at present utterly remote from the reality, might be produced by economic self-government. We may concede that by such means a very large proportion of the necessary work of the world could ultimately be made sufficiently agreeable to be preferred before idleness even by men whose bare livelihood would be assured whether they worked or not. As to the residue let us admit that special rewards, whether in goods or honors or privileges, would have to be given to those who undertook it. But this need not cause any fundamental objection.

There would, of course, be a certain proportion of the population who would prefer idleness. Provided the proportion were small, this need not matter.

And among those who would be classed as idlers might be included artists, writers of books, men devoted to abstract intellectual pursuits—in short, all those whom society despises while they are alive and honors when they are dead. To such men, the possibility of pursuing their own work regardless of any public recognition of its utility would be invaluable. Whoever will observe how many of our poets have been men of private means will realize how much poetic capacity must have remained undeveloped through poverty; for it would be absurd to suppose that the rich are better endowed by nature with the capacity for poetry. Freedom for such men, few as they are, must be set against the waste of the mere idlers.

So far, we have set forth the arguments in favor of the Anarchist plan. They are, to my mind, sufficient to make it seem *possible* that the plan might succeed, but not sufficient to make it so probable that it would be wise to try it.

The question of the feasibility of the Anarchist proposals in regard to distribution is, like so many other questions, a quantitative one. The Anarchist proposals consist of two parts: (1) That all the common commodities should be supplied *ad lib.* to all applicants; (2) That no obligation to work, or economic reward for work, should be imposed on anyone.

These two proposals are not necessarily inseparable, nor does either entail the whole system of Anarchism, though without them Anarchism would hardly be possible. As regards the first of these proposals, it can be carried out even now with regard to some commodities, and it could be carried out in no very distant future with regard to many more. It is a flexible plan, since this or that article of consumption could be placed on the free list or taken off as circumstances might dictate. Its advantages are many and various, and the practice of the world tends to develop in this direction. I think we may conclude that this part of the Anarchists' system might well be adopted bit by bit, reaching gradually the full extension that they desire.

But as regards the second proposal, that there should be no obligation to work, and no economic reward for work, the matter is much more doubtful. Anarchists always assume that if their schemes were put into operation practically everyone would work; but although there is very much more to be said for this view than most people would concede at first sight, yet it is questionable whether there is enough to be said to make it true for practical purposes. Perhaps, in a community where industry had become habitual through economic pressure, public opinion might be sufficiently powerful to compel most men to work;[1] but it is always doubtful how far such a state of things would be permanent. If public opinion is to be really effective, it will be necessary to have some method of dividing the community into small groups, and to allow each group to consume only the equivalent of what it produces. This will make the economic motive operative upon the group, which, since we are supposing it small, will feel that its collective share is appreciably diminished by each idle individual. Such a system might be feasible, but it would be contrary to the whole spirit of Anarchism and would destroy the main lines of its economic system.

The attitude of orthodox Socialism on this question is quite different from that of Anarchism.[2]

---

[1] "As to the so-often repeated objection that nobody would labor if he were not compelled to do so by sheer necessity, we heard enough of it before the emancipation of slaves in America, as well as before the emancipation of serfs in Russia; and we have had the opportunity of appreciating it at its just value. So we shall not try to convince those who can be convinced only by accomplished facts. As to those who reason, they ought to know that, if it really was so with some parts of humanity at its lowest stages—and yet, what do we know about it?—or if it is so with some small communities, or separate individuals, brought to sheer despair by ill-success in their struggle against unfavorable conditions, it is not so with the bulk of the civilized nations. With us, work is a habit, and idleness an artificial growth." Kropotkin, "Anarchist Communism," p. 30.

[2] "While holding this synthetic view on production, the Anarchists cannot consider, like the Collectivists, that a remuneration which would be proportionate to the hours of labor spent by each person in the production of riches may be an ideal, or even an approach to an ideal, society." Kropotkin, "Anarchist Communism;" p. 20.

WORK AND PAY

Among the more immediate measures advocated in the "Communist Manifesto" is "equal liability of all to labor. Establishment of industrial armies, especially for agriculture." The Socialist theory is that, in general, work alone gives the right to the enjoyment of the produce of work. To this theory there will, of course, be exceptions: the old and the very young, the infirm and those whose work is temporarily not required through no fault of their own. But the fundamental conception of Socialism, in regard to our present question, is that all who can should be compelled to work, either by the threat of starvation or by the operation of the criminal law. And, of course, the only kind of work recognized will be such as commends itself to the authorities. Writing books against Socialism, or against any theory embodied in the government of the day, would certainly not be recognized as work. No more would the painting of pictures in a different style from that of the Royal Academy, or producing plays unpleasing to the censor. Any new line of thought would be banned, unless by influence or corruption the thinker could crawl into the good graces of the pundits. These results are not foreseen by Socialists, because they imagine that the Socialist State will be governed by men like those who now advocate it. This is, of course, a delusion. The rulers of the State then will bear as little resemblance to the present Socialists as the dignitaries of the Church after the time of Constantine bore to the Apostles. The men who advocate an unpopular reform are exceptional in disinterestedness and zeal for the public good; but those who hold power after the reform has been carried out are likely to belong, in the main, to the ambitious executive type which has in all ages possessed itself of the government of nations. And this type has never shown itself tolerant of opposition or friendly to freedom.

It would seem, then, that if the Anarchist plan has its dangers, the Socialist plan has at least equal dangers. It is true that the evils we have been foreseeing under Socialism exist at present, but the purpose of Socialists is to cure the evils of the world as it is; they cannot be content with the argument that they would make things no worse.

Anarchism has the advantage as regards liberty, Socialism as regards the inducements to work. Can we not find a method of combining these two advantages? It seems to me that we can.

We saw that, provided most people work in moderation, and their work is rendered as productive as science and organization can make it, there is no good reason why the necessaries of life should not be supplied freely to all. Our only serious doubt was as to whether, in an Anarchist *régime*, the motives for work would be sufficiently powerful to prevent a dangerously large amount of idleness. But it would be easy to decree that, though necessaries should be free to all, whatever went beyond necessaries should only be given to those who were willing to work—not, as is usual at present, only to those in work at any moment, but also to all those who, when they happened not to be working, were idle through no fault of their own. We find at present that a man who has a small income from investments, just sufficient to keep him from actual want, almost always prefers to find some paid work in order to be able to afford luxuries. So it would be, presumably, in such a community as we are imagining. At the same time, the man who felt a vocation for some unrecognized work of art or science or thought would be free to follow his desire, provided he were willing to " scorn delights and live laborious days." And the comparatively small number of men with an invincible horror of work—the sort of men who now become tramps—might lead a harmless existence, without any grave danger of their becoming sufficiently numerous to be a serious burden upon the more industrious. In this way, the claims of freedom could be combined with the need of some economic stimulus to work. Such a system, it seems to me, would have a far greater chance of success than either pure Anarchism or pure orthodox Socialism.

Stated in more familiar terms, the plan we are

advocating amounts essentially to this: that a certain small income, sufficient for necessaries, should be secured to all, whether they work or not, and that a larger income, as much larger as might be warranted by the total amount of commodities produced, should be given to those who are willing to engage in some work which the community recognizes as useful. On this basis we may build further. I do not think it is always necessary to pay more highly work which is more skilled or regarded as socially more useful, since such work is more interesting and more respected than ordinary work, and will therefore often be preferred by those who are able to do it. But we might, for instance, give an intermediate income to those who are only willing to work half the usual number of hours, and an income above that of most workers to those who choose a specially disagreeable trade. Such a system is perfectly compatible with Socialism, though perhaps hardly with Anarchism. Of its advantages we shall have more to say at a later stage. For the present I am content to urge that it combines freedom with justice, and avoids those dangers to the community which we have found to lurk both in the proposals of the Anarchists and in those of orthodox Socialists.

CHAPTER V

GOVERNMENT AND LAW

GOVERNMENT and Law, in their very essence, consist of restrictions on freedom, and freedom is the greatest of political goods.[1] A hasty reasoner might conclude without further ado that Law and government are evils which must be abolished if freedom is our goal. But this consequence, true or false, cannot be proved so simply. In this chapter we shall examine the arguments of Anarchists against law and the State. We shall proceed on the assumption that freedom is the supreme aim of a good social system; but on this very basis we shall find the Anarchist contentions very questionable.

Respect for the liberty of others is not a natural impulse with most men: envy and love of power lead ordinary human nature to find pleasure in interferences with the lives of others. If all men's actions were wholly unchecked by external authority, we should not obtain a world in which all men would be

---

[1] I do not say freedom is the greatest of *all* goods: the best things come from within—they are such things as creative art, and love, and thought. Such things can be helped or hindered by political conditions, but not actually produced by them; and freedom is, both in itself and in its relation to these other goods, the best thing that political and economic conditions can secure.

111

free. The strong would oppress the weak, or the majority would oppress the minority, or the lovers of violence would oppress the more peaceable people. I fear it cannot be said that these bad impulses are *wholly* due to a bad social system, though it must be conceded that the present competitive organization of society does a great deal to foster the worst elements in human nature. The love of power is an impulse which, though innate in very ambitious men, is chiefly promoted as a rule by the actual experience of power. In a world where none could acquire much power, the desire to tyrannize would be much less strong than it is at present. Nevertheless, I cannot think that it would be wholly absent, and those in whom it would exist would often be men of unusual energy and executive capacity. Such men, if they are not restrained by the organized will of the community, may either succeed in establishing a despotism, or, at any rate, make such a vigorous attempt as can only be defeated through a period of prolonged disturbance. And apart from the love or political power, there is the love of power over individuals. If threats and terrorism were not prevented by law, it can hardly be doubted that cruelty would be rife in the relations of men and women, and of parents and children. It is true that the habits of a community can make such cruelty rare, but these

GOVERNMENT AND LAW

habits, I fear, are only to be produced through the prolonged reign of law. Experience of backwoods communities, mining camps and other such places seems to show that under new conditions men easily revert to a more barbarous attitude and practice. It would seem, therefore, that, while human nature remains as it is, there will be more liberty for all in a community where some acts of tyranny by individuals are forbidden, than in a community where the law leaves each individual free to follow his every impulse. But, although the necessity of some form of government and law must for the present be conceded, it is important to remember that all law and government is in itself in some degree an evil, only justifiable when it prevents other and greater evils. Every use of the power of the State needs, therefore, to be very closely scrutinized, and every possibility of diminishing its power is to be welcomed provided it does not lead to a reign of private tyranny.

The power of the State is partly legal, partly economic: acts of a kind which the State dislikes can be punished by the criminal law, and individuals who incur the displeasure of the State may find it hard to earn a livelihood.

The views of Marx on the State are not very clear. On the one hand he seems willing, like the modern State Socialists, to allow great power to the

State, but on the other hand he suggests that when the Socialist revolution has been consummated, the State, as we know it, will disappear. Among the measures which are advocated in the Communist Manifesto as immediately desirable, there are several which would very greatly increase the power of the existing State. For example, "Centralization of credit in the hands of the State, by means of a national bank with State capital and an exclusive monopoly;" and again, "Centralization of the means of communication and transport in the hands of the State." But the Manifesto goes on to say:

When, in the course of development, class distinctions have disappeared, and all production has been concentrated in the hands of a vast association of the whole nation, the public power will lose its political character. Political power, properly so called, is merely the organised power of one class for oppressing another. If the proletariat during its contest with the bourgeoisie is compelled, by the force of circumstances, to organize itself as a class, if, by means of a revolution, it makes itself the ruling class, and, as such, sweeps away by force the old conditions of production, then it will, along with these conditions, have swept away the conditions for the existence of class antagonisms, and of classes generally, and will thereby have abolished its own supremacy as a class.

In place of the old bourgeois society, with its classes and class antagonisms, we shall have an association, in

GOVERNMENT AND LAW 115

which the free development of each is the condition for the free development of all.[1]

This attitude Marx preserved in essentials throughout his life. Accordingly, it is not to be wondered at that his followers, so far as regards their immediate aims, have in the main become out-and-out State Socialists. On the other hand, the Syndicalists, who accept from Marx the doctrine of the class war, which they regard as what is really vital in his teaching, reject the State with abhorrence and wish to abolish it wholly, in which respect they are at one with the Anarchists. The Guild Socialists, though some persons in this country regard them as extremists, really represent the English love of compromise. The Syndicalist arguments as to the dangers inherent in the power of the State have made them dissatisfied with the old State Socialism, but they are unable to accept the Anarchist view that society can dispense altogether with a central authority. Accordingly they propose that there should be two co-equal instruments of Government in a community, the one geographical, representing the consumers, and essentially the continuation of the democratic State; the other representing the producers, organized, not geographically, but in guilds, after the manner of industrial unionism. These two author-

---
[1] Communist Manifesto, p. 22.

ities will deal with different classes of questions. Guild Socialists do not regard the industrial authority as forming part of the State, for they contend that it is the essence of the State to be geographical; but the industrial authority will resemble the present State in the fact that it will have coercive powers, and that its decrees will be enforced, when necessary. It is to be suspected that Syndicalists also, much as they object to the existing State, would not object to coercion of individuals in an industry by the Trade Union in that industry. Government within the Trade Union would probably be quite as strict as State government is now. In saying this we are assuming that the theoretical Anarchism of Syndicalist leaders would not survive accession to power, but I am afraid experience shows that this is not a very hazardous assumption.

Among all these different views, the one which raises the deepest issue is the Anarchist contention that all coercion by the community is unnecessary. Like most of the things that Anarchists say, there is much more to be urged in support of this view than most people would suppose at first sight. Kropotkin, who is its ablest exponent, points out how much has been achieved already by the method of free agreement. He does not wish to abolish government in the sense of collective decisions: what he does wish to abolish is the system by which a decision is en-

GOVERNMENT AND LAW 117

forced upon those who oppose it.[1] The whole system of representative government and majority rule is to him a bad thing.[2] He points to such instances as the agreements among the different railway systems of the Continent for the running of through expresses and for co-operation generally. He points out that in such cases the different companies or authorities concerned each appoint a delegate, and that the delegates suggest a basis of agreement, which has to be subsequently ratified by each of the bodies ap-

---

[1] "On the other hand, the *State* has also been confused with *government*. As there can be no State without government, it has been sometimes said that it is the absence of government, and not the abolition of the State, that should be the aim.

"It seems to me, however, that State and government represent two ideas of a different kind. The State idea implies quite another idea to that of government. It not only includes the existence of a power placed above society, but also a *territorial concentration* and a *concentration of many functions of the life of society in the hands of a few or even of all*. It implies new relations among the members of society.

"This characteristic distinction, which perhaps escapes notice at first sight, appears clearly when the origin of the State is studied." Kropotkin, "The State." p. 4.

[2] "Representative government has accomplished its historical mission; it has given a mortal blow to Court-rule; and by its debates it has awakened public interest in public questions. But, to see in it the government of the future Socialist society, is to commit a gross error. Each economical phase of life implies its own political phase; and it is impossible to touch the very basis of the present economical life—private property—without a corresponding change in the very basis of the political organization. Life already shows in which direction the change will be made. Not in increasing the powers of the State, but in resorting to free organization and free federation in all those branches which are now considered as attributes of the State." Kropotkin, "Anarchist Communism," pp. 28-29.

pointing them. The assembly of delegates has no
coercive power whatever, and a majority can do
nothing against a recalcitrant minority. Yet this has
not prevented the conclusion of very elaborate systems of agreements. By such methods, so Anarchists
contend, the *useful* functions of government can be
carried out without any coercion. They maintain
that the usefulness of agreement is so patent as to
make co-operation certain if once the predatory
motives associated with the present system of private
property were removed.

Attractive as this view is, I cannot resist the conclusion that it results from impatience and represents the attempt to find a short-cut toward the
ideal which all humane people desire.

Let us begin with the question of private crime.[1]
Anarchists maintain that the criminal is manufactured by bad social conditions and would disappear
in such a world as they aim at creating.[2] No doubt

---

[1] On this subject there is an excellent discussion in the before-mentioned work of Monsieur Naquet.

[2] "As to the third—the chief—objection, which maintains the necessity of a government for punishing those who break the law of society, there is so much to say about it that it hardly can be touched incidentally. The more we study the question, the more we are brought to the conclusion that society itself is responsible for the anti-social deeds perpetrated in its midst, and that no punishment, no prisons, and no hangmen can diminish the numbers of such deeds; nothing short of a reorganization of society itself. Three-quarters of all the acts which are brought every year before our courts have their origin, either directly or indirectly, in the present disorganized state of society with

GOVERNMENT AND LAW 119

there is a great measure of truth in this view. There would be little motive to robbery, for example, in an Anarchist world, unless it were organized on a large scale by a body of men bent on upsetting the Anarchist *régime*. It may also be conceded that impulses toward criminal violence could be very largely eliminated by a better education. But all such contentions, it seems to me, have their limitations. To take an extreme case, we cannot suppose that there would be no lunatics in an Anarchist community, and some of these lunatics would, no doubt, be homicidal. Probably no one would argue that they ought to be left at liberty. But there are no sharp lines in nature; from the homicidal lunatic to the sane man of violent passions there is a continuous gradation. Even in the most perfect community there will be men and women, otherwise sane, who will feel an impulse to commit murder from jealousy. These are now usually restrained by the fear of punishment,

---

regard to the production and distribution of wealth—not in the perversity of human nature. As to the relatively few anti-social deeds which result from anti-social inclinations of separate individuals, it is not by prisons, nor even by resorting to the hangmen, that we can diminish their numbers. By our prisons, we merely multiply them and render them worse. By our detectives, our 'price of blood,' our executions, and our jails, we spread in society such a terrible flow of basest passions and habits, that he who should realize the effects of these institutions to their full extent, would be frightened by what society is doing under the pretext of maintaining morality. We *must* search for other remedies, and the remedies have been indicated long since." Kropotkin, "Anarchist Communism," pp. 31-32.

but if this fear were removed, such murders would probably become much more common, as may be seen from the present behavior of certain soldiers on leave. Moreover, certain kinds of conduct arouse public hostility, and would almost inevitably lead to lynching, if no other recognized method of punishment existed. There is in most men a certain natural vindictiveness, not always directed against the worst members of the community. For example, Spinoza was very nearly murdered by the mob because he was suspected of undue friendliness to France at a time when Holland was at war with that country. Apart from such cases, there would be the very real danger of an organized attempt to destroy Anarchism and revive ancient oppressions. Is it to be supposed, for example, that Napoleon, if he had been born into such a community as Kropotkin advocates, would have acquiesced tamely in a world where his genius could find no scope? I cannot see what should prevent a combination of ambitious men forming themselves into a private army, manufacturing their own munitions, and at last enslaving the defenseless citizens, who had relied upon the inherent attractiveness of liberty. It would not be consistent with the principles of Anarchism for the community to interfere with the drilling of a private army, no matter what its objects might be (though, of course, an opposing private army might be formed by men with different

GOVERNMENT AND LAW

views). Indeed, Kropotkin instances the old volunteers in Great Britain as an example of a movement on Anarchist lines.[1] Even if a predatory army were not formed from within, it might easily come from a neighboring nation, or from races on the borderland of civilization. So long as the love of power exists, I do not see how it can be prevented from finding an outlet in oppression except by means of the organized force of the community.

The conclusion, which appears to be forced upon us, is that the Anarchist ideal of a community in which no acts are forbidden by law is not, at any rate for the present, compatible with the stability of such a world as the Anarchists desire. In order to obtain and preserve a world resembling as closely as possible that at which they aim, it will still be necessary that some acts should be forbidden by law. We may put the chief of these under three heads:

1. Theft.
2. Crimes of violence.
3. The creation of organizations intended to subvert the Anarchist *régime* by force.

We will briefly recapitulate what has been said already as to the necessity of these prohibitions.

1. *Theft.*—It is true that in an Anarchist world

---

[1] "Anarchist Communism," p. 27.

there will be no destitution, and therefore no thefts motived by starvation. But such thefts are at present by no means the most considerable or the most harmful. The system of rationing, which is to be applied to luxuries, will leave many men with fewer luxuries than they might desire. It will give opportunities for peculation by those who are in control of the public stores, and it will leave the possibility of appropriating such valuable objects of art as would naturally be preserved in public museums. It may be contended that such forms of theft would be prevented by public opinion. But public opinion is not greatly operative upon an individual unless it is the opinion of his own group. A group of men combined for purposes of theft might readily defy the public opinion of the majority unless that public opinion made itself effective by the use of force against them. Probably, in fact, such force would be applied through popular indignation, but in that case we should revive the evils of the criminal law with the added evils of uncertainty, haste and passion, which are inseparable from the practice of lynching. If, as we have suggested, it were found necessary to provide an economic stimulus to work by allowing fewer luxuries to idlers, this would afford a new motive for theft on their part and a new necessity for some form of criminal law.

2. *Crimes of Violence.*—Cruelty to children,

crimes of jealousy, rape, and so forth, are almost certain to occur in any society to some extent. The prevention of such acts is essential to the existence of freedom for the weak. If nothing were done to hinder them, it is to be feared that the customs of a society would gradually become rougher, and that acts which are now rare would cease to be so. If Anarchists are right in maintaining that the existence of such an economic system as they desire would prevent the commission of crimes of this kind, the laws forbidding them would no longer come into operation, and would do no harm to liberty. If, on the other hand, the impulse to such actions persisted, it would be necessary that steps should be taken to restrain men from indulging it.

3. The third class of difficulties is much the most serious and involves much the most drastic interference with liberty. I do not see how a private army could be tolerated within an Anarchist community, and I do not see how it could be prevented except by a general prohibition of carrying arms. If there were no such prohibition, rival parties would organize rival forces, and civil war would result. Yet, if there is such a prohibition, it cannot well be carried out without a very considerable interference with individual liberty. No doubt, after a time, the idea of using violence to achieve a political object might die down, as the practice of duelling has done. But such

changes of habit and outlook are facilitated by legal prohibition, and would hardly come about without it. I shall not speak yet of the international aspect of this same problem, for I propose to deal with that in the next chapter, but it is clear that the same considerations apply with even greater force to the relations between nations.

If we admit, however reluctantly, that a criminal law is necessary and that the force of the community must be brought to bear to prevent certain kinds of actions, a further question arises: How is crime to be treated? What is the greatest measure of humanity and respect for freedom that is compatible with the recognition of such a thing as crime? The first thing to recognize is that the whole conception of guilt or sin should be utterly swept away. At present, the criminal is visited with the displeasure of the community: the sole method applied to prevent the occurrence of crime is the infliction of pain upon the criminal. Everything possible is done to break his spirit and destroy his self-respect. Even those pleasures which would be most likely to have a civilizing effect are forbidden to him, merely on the ground that they are pleasures, while much of the suffering inflicted is of a kind which can only brutalize and degrade still further. I am not speaking, of course, of those few penal institutions which have made a serious study of reforming the criminal. Such institutions, especially in America, have been proved capable of achieving the most remarkable results, but they remain everywhere exceptional. The broad rule is still that the criminal is made to feel the displeasure of society. He must emerge from such a treatment either defiant and hostile, or submissive and cringing, with a broken spirit and a loss of self-respect. Neither of these results is anything but evil. Nor can any good result be achieved by a method of treatment which embodies reprobation.

When a man is suffering from an infectious disease he is a danger to the community, and it is necessary to restrict his liberty of movement. But no one associates any idea of guilt with such a situation. On the contrary, he is an object of commiseration to his friends. Such steps as science recommends are taken to cure him of his disease, and he submits as a rule without reluctance to the curtailment of liberty involved meanwhile. The same method in spirit ought to be shown in the treatment of what is called "crime." It is supposed, of course, that the criminal is actuated by calculations of self-interest, and that the fear of punishment, by supplying a contrary motive of self-interest affords the best deterrent.

> The dog, to gain some private end,
> Went mad and bit the man.

This is the popular view of crime; yet no dog goes mad from choice, and probably the same is true of the great majority of criminals, certainly in the case of crimes of passion. Even in cases where self-interest is the motive, the important thing is to prevent the crime, not to make the criminal suffer. Any suffering which may be entailed by the process of prevention ought to be regarded as regrettable, like the pain involved in a surgical operation. The man who commits a crime from an impulse to violence ought to be subjected to a scientific psychological treatment, designed to elicit more beneficial impulses. The man who commits a crime from calculations of self-interest ought to be made to feel that self-interest itself, when it is fully understood, can be better served by a life which is useful to the community than by one which is harmful. For this purpose it is chiefly necessary to widen his outlook and increase the scope of his desires. At present, when a man suffers from insufficient love for his fellow-creatures, the method of curing him which is commonly adopted seems scarcely designed to succeed, being, indeed, in essentials, the same as his attitude toward them. The object of the prison administration is to save trouble, not to study the individual case. He is kept in captivity in a cell from which all sight of the earth is shut out: he is subjected to harshness by warders, who have too often become brutalized by their occupation.[1] He is solemnly denounced as an enemy to society. He is compelled to perform mechanical tasks, chosen for their wearisomeness. He is given no education and no incentive to self-improvement. Is it to be wondered at if, at the end of such a course of treatment, his feelings toward the community are no more friendly than they were at the beginning?

Severity of punishment arose through vindictiveness and fear in an age when many criminals escaped justice altogether, and it was hoped that savage sentences would outweigh the chance of escape in the mind of the criminal. At present a very large part of the criminal law is concerned in safeguarding the rights of property, that is to say—as things are now—the unjust privileges of the rich. Those whose principles lead them into conflict with government, like Anarchists, bring a most formidable indictment against the law and the authorities for the unjust manner in which they support the *status quo*. Many of the actions by which men have become rich are far more harmful to the community than the obscure crimes of poor men, yet they go unpunished because they do not interfere with the existing order. If the power of the community is to be brought to bear to prevent certain classes of actions through the agency

---

[1] This was written before the author had any personal experience of the prison system. He personally met with nothing but kindness at the hands of the prison officials.

of the criminal law, it is as necessary that these actions should really be those which are harmful to the community, as it is that the treatment of "criminals" should be freed from the conception of guilt and inspired by the same spirit as is shown in the treatment of disease. But, if these two conditions were fulfilled, I cannot help thinking that a society which preserved the existence of law would be preferable to one conducted on the unadulterated principles of Anarchism.

So far we have been considering the power which the State derives from the criminal law. We have every reason to think that this power cannot be entirely abolished, though it can be exercised in a wholly different spirit, without the vindictiveness and the moral reprobation which now form its essence.

We come next to the consideration of the economic power of the State and the influence which it can exert through its bureaucracy. State Socialists argue as if there would be no danger to liberty in a State not based upon capitalism. This seems to me an entire delusion. Given an official caste, however selected, there are bound to be a set of men whose whole instincts will drive them toward tyranny. Together with the natural love of power, they will have a rooted conviction (visible now in the higher ranks of the Civil Service) that they alone know enough to be able to judge what is for the good of the community. Like all men who administer a system, they will come to feel the system itself sacrosanct. The only changes they will desire will be changes in the direction of further regulations as to how the people are to enjoy the good things kindly granted to them by their benevolent despots. Whoever thinks this picture overdrawn must have failed to study the influence and methods of Civil Servants at present. On every matter that arises, they know far more than the general public about all the *definite* facts involved; the one thing they do not know is " where the shoe pinches." But those who know this are probably not skilled in stating their case, not able to say off-hand exactly how many shoes are pinching how many feet, or what is the precise remedy required. The answer prepared for Ministers by the Civil Service is accepted by the " respectable " public as impartial, and is regarded as disposing of the case of malcontents except on a first-class political question on which elections may be won or lost. That at least is the way in which things are managed in England. And there is every reason to fear that under State Socialism the power of officials would be vastly greater than it is at present.

Those who accept the orthodox doctrine of democracy contend that, if ever the power of capital were removed, representative institutions would suffice to undo the evils threatened by bureaucracy. Against this view, Anarchists and Syndicalists have directed a merciless criticism. French Syndicalists especially, living, as they do, in a highly democratized country, have had bitter experience of the way in which the power of the State can be employed against a progressive minority. This experience has led them to abandon altogether the belief in the divine right of majorities. The Constitution that they would desire would be one which allowed scope for vigorous minorities, conscious of their aims and prepared to work for them. It is undeniable that, to all who care for progress, actual experience of democratic representative Government is very disillusioning. Admitting—as I think we must—that it is preferable to any *previous* form of Government, we must yet acknowledge that much of the criticism directed against it by Anarchists and Syndicalists is thoroughly justified.

Such criticism would have had more influence if any clear idea of an alternative to parliamentary democracy had been generally apprehended. But it must be confessed that Syndicalists have not presented their case in a way which is likely to attract the average citizen. Much of what they say amounts to this: that a minority, consisting of skilled workers in vital industries, can, by a strike, make the economic life of the whole community impossible, and can in this way force their will upon the nation. The action aimed at is compared to the seizure of a power-station, by which a whole vast system can be paralyzed. Such a doctrine is an appeal to force, and is naturally met by an appeal to force on the other side. It is useless for the Syndicalists to protest that they only desire power in order to promote liberty: the world which they are seeking to establish does not, as yet, appeal to the effective will of the community, and cannot be stably inaugurated until it does do so. Persuasion is a slow process, and may sometimes be accelerated by violent methods; to this extent such methods may be justified. But the ultimate goal of any reformer who aims at liberty can only be reached through persuasion. The attempt to thrust liberty by force upon those who do not desire what we consider liberty must always prove a failure; and Syndicalists, like other reformers, must ultimately rely upon persuasion for success.

But it would be a mistake to confuse aims with methods: however little we may agree with the proposal to force the millennium on a reluctant community by starvation, we may yet agree that much of what the Syndicalists desire to achieve is desirable.

Let us dismiss from our minds such criticisms of parliamentary government as are bound up with the present system of private property, and consider only those which would remain true in a collectivist community. Certain defects seem inherent in the very nature of representative institutions. There is a sense of self-importance, inseparable from success in a contest for popular favor. There is an all-but unavoidable habit of hypocrisy, since experience shows that the democracy does not detect insincerity in an orator, and will, on the other hand, be shocked by things which even the most sincere men may think necessary. Hence arises a tone of cynicism among elected representatives, and a feeling that no man can retain his position in politics without deceit. This is as much the fault of the democracy as of the representatives, but it seems unavoidable so long as the main thing that all bodies of men demand of their champions is flattery. However the blame may be apportioned, the evil must be recognized as one which is bound to occur in the existing forms of democracy. Another evil, which is especially noticeable in large States, is the remoteness of the seat of government from many of the constituencies—a remoteness which is psychological even more than geographical. The legislators live in comfort, protected by thick walls and innumerable policemen from the voice of the mob; as time goes on they remember only dimly the passions and promises of their electoral campaign; they come to feel it an essential part of statesmanship to consider what are called the interests of the community as a whole, rather than those of some discontented group; but the interests of the community as a whole are sufficiently vague to be easily seen to

GOVERNMENT AND LAW 133

coincide with self-interest. All these causes lead Parliaments to betray the people, consciously or unconsciously; and it is no wonder if they have produced a certain aloofness from democratic theory in the more vigorous champions of labor.

Majority rule, as it exists in large States, is subject to the fatal defect that, in a very great number of questions, only a fraction of the nation have any direct interest or knowledge, yet the others have an equal voice in their settlement. When people have no direct interest in a question they are very apt to be influenced by irrelevant considerations; this is shown in the extraordinary reluctance to grant autonomy to subordinate nations or groups. For this reason, it is very dangerous to allow the nation as a whole to decide on matters which concern only a small section, whether that section be geographical or industrial or defined in any other way. The best cure for this evil, so far as can be seen at present, lies in allowing self-government to every important group within a nation in all matters that affect that group much more than they affect the rest of the community. The government of a group, chosen by the group, will be far more in touch with its constituents, far more conscious of their interests, than a remote Parliament nominally representing the whole country. The most original idea in Syndicalism—adopted and developed by the Guild Socialists—is the idea of making industries self-governing units so far as their internal affairs are concerned. By this method, extended also to such other groups as have clearly separable interests, the evils which have shown themselves in representative democracy can, I believe, be largely overcome.

Guild Socialists, as we have seen, have another suggestion, growing naturally out of the autonomy of industrial guilds, by which they hope to limit the power of the State and help to preserve individual liberty. They propose that, in addition to Parliament, elected (as at present) on a territorial basis and representing the community as consumers, there shall also be a " Guild Congress," a glorified successor of the present Trade Union Congress, which shall consist of representatives chosen by the Guilds, and shall represent the community as producers.

This method of diminishing the excessive power of the State has been attractively set forth by Mr. G. D. H. Cole in his " Self-Government in Industry."[1] " Where now," he says, " the State passes a Factory Act, or a Coal Mines Regulation Act, the Guild Congress of the future will pass such Acts, and its power of enforcing them will be the same as that of the State " (p. 98). His ultimate ground for advocating this system is that, in his opinion, it will tend to preserve individual liberty: " The fundamental reason

---
[1] Bell, 1917.

for the preservation, in a democratic Society, of both the industrial and the political forms of Social organization is, it seems to me, that only by dividing the vast power now wielded by industrial capitalism can the individual hope to be free " (p. 91).

Will the system suggested by Mr. Cole have this result? I think it is clear that it would, in this respect, be an improvement on the existing system. Representative government cannot but be improved by any method which brings the representatives into closer touch with the interests concerned in their legislation; and this advantage probably would be secured by handing over questions of production to the Guild Congress. But if, in spite of the safeguards proposed by the Guild Socialists, the Guild Congress became all-powerful in such questions, if resistance to its will by a Guild which felt ill-used became practically hopeless, I fear that the evils now connected with the omnipotence of the State would soon reappear. Trade Union officials, as soon as they become part of the governing forces in the country, tend to become autocratic and conservative; they lose touch with their constituents and gravitate, by a psychological sympathy, into co-operation with the powers that be. Their formal installation in authority through the Guilds Congress would accelerate this process. They would soon tend to combine, in effect if not obviously, with those who wield authority in

Parliament. Apart from occasional conflicts, comparable to the rivalry of opposing financiers which now sometimes disturbs the harmony of the capitalist world, there would, at most times, be agreement between the dominant personalities in the two Houses. And such harmony would filch away from the individual the liberty which he had hoped to secure by the quarrels of his masters.

There is no method, if we are not mistaken, by which a body representing the whole community, whether as producers or consumers or both, can alone be a sufficient guardian of individual liberty. The only way of preserving sufficient liberty (and even this will be inadequate in the case of very small minorities) is the organization of citizens with special interests into groups, determined to preserve autonomy as regards their internal affairs, willing to resist interference by a strike if necessary, and sufficiently powerful (either in themselves or through their power of appealing to public sympathy) to be able to resist the organized forces of government successfully when their cause is such as many men think just. If this method is to be successful we must have not only suitable organizations but also a diffused respect for liberty, and an absence of submissiveness to government both in theory and practice. Some risk of disorder there must be in such a society, but this risk is as nothing compared to the

GOVERNMENT AND LAW

danger of stagnation which is inseparable from an all-powerful central authority.

We may now sum up our discussion of the powers of Government.

The State, in spite of what Anarchists urge, seems a necessary institution for certain purposes. Peace and war, tariffs, regulation of sanitary conditions and of the sale of noxious drugs, the preservation of a just system of distribution: these, among others, are functions which could hardly be performed in a community in which there was no central government. Take, for example, the liquor traffic, or the opium traffic in China. If alcohol could be obtained at cost price without taxation, still more if it could be obtained for nothing, as Anarchists presumably desire, can we believe that there would not be a great and disastrous increase of drunkenness? China was brought to the verge of ruin by opium, and every patriotic Chinaman desired to see the traffic in opium restricted. In such matters freedom is not a panacea, and some degree of legal restriction seems imperative for the national health.

But granting that the State, in some form, must continue, we must also grant, I think, that its powers ought to be very strictly limited to what is absolutely necessary. There is no way of limiting its powers except by means of groups which are jealous of their privileges and determined to preserve their autonomy, even if this should involve resistance to laws decreed by the State, when these laws interfere in the internal affairs of a group in ways not warranted by the public interest. The glorification of the State, and the doctrine that it is every citizen's duty to serve the State, are radically against progress and against liberty. The State, though at present a source of much evil, is also a means to certain good things, and will be needed so long as violent and destructive impulses remain common. But it is *merely* a means, and a means which needs to be very carefully and sparingly used if it is not to do more harm than good. It is not the State, but the community, the world-wide community of all human beings present and future, that we ought to serve. And a good community does not spring from the glory of the State, but from the unfettered development of individuals: from happiness in daily life, from congenial work giving opportunity for whatever constructiveness each man or woman may possess, from free personal relations embodying love and taking away the roots of envy in thwarted capacity from affection, and above all from the joy of life and its expression in the spontaneous creations of art and science. It is these things that make an age or a nation worthy of existence, and these things are not to be secured by bowing down before the State. It is the individual in whom all that is good must be realized, and the free growth of the individual must be the supreme end of a political system which is to re-fashion the world.

CHAPTER VI

INTERNATIONAL RELATIONS

The main objects which should be served by international relations may be taken to be two: First, the avoidance of wars, and, second, the prevention of the oppression of weak nations by strong ones. These two objects do not by any means necessarily lead in the same direction, since one of the easiest ways of securing the world's peace would be by a combination of the most powerful States for the exploitation and oppression of the remainder. This method, however, is not one which the lover of liberty can favor. We must keep account of both aims and not be content with either alone.

One of the commonplaces of both Socialism and Anarchism is that all modern wars are due to capitalism, and would cease if capitalism were abolished. This view, to my mind, is only a half-truth; the half that is true is important, but the half that is untrue is perhaps equally important when a fundamental reconstruction of society is being considered.

Socialist and Anarchist critics of existing society point, with perfect truth, to certain capitalistic factors which promote war. The first of these is the desire of finance to find new fields of investment in undeveloped countries. Mr. J. A. Hobson, an author who is by no means extreme in his views, has well stated this point in his book on "The Evolution of Modern Capitalism."[1] He says:

The economic tap-root, the chief directing motive of all the modern imperialistic expansion, is the pressure of capitalist industries for markets, primarily markets for investment, secondarily markets for surplus products of home industry. Where the concentration of capital has gone furthest, and where a rigorous protective system prevails, this pressure is necessarily strongest. Not merely do the trusts and other manufacturing trades that restrict their output for the home market more urgently require foreign markets, but they are also more anxious to secure protected markets, and this can only be achieved by extending the area of political rule. This is the essential significance of the recent change in American foreign policy as illustrated by the Spanish War, the Philippine annexation, the Panama policy, and the new application of the Monroe doctrine to the South American States. South America is needed as a preferential market for investment of trust "profits" and surplus trust products: if in time these states can be brought within a Zollverein under the suzerainty of the United States, the financial area of operations receives a notable accession. China as a field of railway enterprise and general industrial development already begins to loom large in the eyes of

---

[1] Walter Scott Publishing Company, 1906, p. 262.

foresighted American business men; the growing trade in American cotton and other goods in that country will be a subordinate consideration to the expansion of the area for American investments. Diplomatic pressure, armed force, and, where desirable, seizure of territory for political control, will be engineered by the financial magnates who control the political destiny of America. The strong and expensive American navy now beginning to be built incidentally serves the purpose of affording profitable contracts to the shipbuilding and metal industries: its real meaning and use is to forward the aggressive political policy imposed upon the nation by the economic needs of the financial capitalists.

It should be clearly understood that this constant pressure to extend the area of markets is not a necessary implication of all forms of organized industry. If competition was displaced by combinations of a genuinely coöperative character in which the whole gain of improved economies passed, either to the workers in wages, or to large bodies of investors in dividends, the expansion of demand in the home markets would be so great as to give full employment to the productive powers of concentrated capital, and there would be no self-accumulating masses of profit expressing themselves in new credit and demanding external employment. It is the " monopoly " profits of trusts and combines, taken either in construction, financial operation, or industrial working, that form a gathering fund of self-accumulating credit whose possession by the financial class implies a contracted demand for commodities and a correspondingly restricted employment for capital in American industries. Within certain limits relief can be found by stimulation of the export trade under cover of a high protective tariff which forbids all interference with monopoly of the home markets. But it is extremely difficult for trusts adapted to the requirements of a profitable tied market at home to adjust their methods of free competition in the world markets upon a profitable basis of steady trading. Moreover, such a mode of expansion is only appropriate to certain manufacturing trusts: the owners of railroad, financial and other trusts must look always more to foreign investments for their surplus profits. This ever-growing need for fresh fields of investment for their profits is the great crux of the financial system, and threatens to dominate the future economics and the politics of the great Republic.

The financial economy of American capitalism exhibits in more dramatic shape a tendency common to the finance of all developed industrial nations. The large, easy flow of capital from Great Britain, Germany, Austria, France, etc., into South African or Australian mines, into Egyptian bonds, or the precarious securities of South American republics, attests the same general pressure which increases with every development of financial machinery and the more profitable control of that machinery by the class of professional financiers.

The kind of way in which such conditions tend toward war might have been illustrated, if Mr. Hobson had been writing at a later date, by various more recent cases. A higher rate of interest is obtainable on enterprises in an undeveloped country than in a developed one, provided the risks connected with an unsettled government can be minimized. To minimize these risks the financiers call in the assistance of the military and naval forces of the country which they are momentarily asserting to be theirs. In order to have the support of public opinion in this demand they have recourse to the power of the Press.

The Press is the second great factor to which critics of capitalism point when they wish to prove that capitalism is the source of modern war. Since the running of a big newspaper requires a large capital, the proprietors of important organs necessarily belong to the capitalist class, and it will be a rare and exceptional event if they do not sympathize with their own class in opinion and outlook. They are able to decide what news the great mass of newspaper readers shall be allowed to have. They can actually falsify the news, or, without going so far as that, they can carefully select it, giving such items as will stimulate the passions which they desire to stimulate, and suppressing such items as would provide the antidote. In this way the picture of the world in the mind of the average newspaper reader is made to be not a true picture, but in the main that which suits the interests of capitalists. This is true in many directions, but above all in what concerns the relations between nations. The mass of the population of a country can be led to love or hate any other country at the will of the newspaper proprietors, which is often, directly or indirectly, influenced by the will of the great financiers. So long as enmity between England and Russia was desired, our newspapers were full of the cruel treatment meted out to Russian political prisoners, the oppression of Finland and Russian Poland, and other such topics. As soon as our foreign policy changed, these items disappeared from the more important newspapers, and we heard instead of the misdeeds of Germany. Most men are not sufficiently critical to be on their guard against such influences, and until they are, the power of the Press will remain.

Besides these two influences of capitalism in promoting war, there is another, much less emphasized by the critics of capitalism, but by no means less important: I mean the pugnacity which tends to be developed in men who have the habit of command. So long as capitalist society persists, an undue measure of power will be in the hands of those who have acquired wealth and influence through a great position in industry or finance. Such men are in the habit, in private life, of finding their will seldom questioned; they are surrounded by obsequious satellites and are not infrequently engaged in conflicts with Trade Unions. Among their friends and acquaintances are included those who hold high positions in government or administration, and these men equally are liable to become autocratic through the habit of giving orders. It used to be customary to speak of the " governing classes," but nominal democracy has caused this phrase to go out of fashion. Nevertheless, it still retains much truth; there are still in any capitalist community those who command and those who as a rule obey. The outlook of these two classes is very different, though in a modern society there is a continuous gradation from the extreme of the one to the extreme of the other. The man who is accustomed to find submission to his will becomes indignant on the occasions when he finds opposition. Instinctively he is convinced that opposition is wicked and must be crushed. He is therefore much more willing than the average citizen to resort to war against his rivals. Accordingly we find, though, of course, with very notable exceptions, that in the main those who have most power are most warlike, and those who have least power are least disposed to hatred of foreign nations. This is one of the evils inseparable from the concentration of power. It will only be cured by the abolition of capitalism if the new system is one which allows very much less power to single individuals. It will not be cured by a system which substitutes the power of Ministers or officials for the power of capitalists.

This is one reason, additional to those mentioned in the preceding chapter, for desiring to see a diminution in the authority of the State.

Not only does the concentration of power tend to cause wars, but, equally, wars and the fear of them bring about the necessity for the concentration of power. So long as the community is exposed to sudden dangers, the possibility of quick decision is absolutely necessary to self-preservation. The cumbrous machinery of deliberative decisions by the people is impossible in a crisis, and therefore so long as crises are likely to occur, it is impossible to abolish the almost autocratic power of governments. In this case, as in most others, each of two correlative evils tends to perpetuate the other. The existence of men with the habit of power increases the risk of war, and the risk of war makes it impossible to establish a system where no man possesses great power.

So far we have been considering what is true in the contention that capitalism causes modern wars. It is time now to look at the other side, and to ask ourselves whether the abolition of capitalism would, by itself, be sufficient to prevent war.

I do not myself believe that this is the case. The outlook of both Socialists and Anarchists seems to me, in this respect as in some others, to be unduly divorced from the fundamental instincts of human nature. There were wars before there was capitalism, and fighting is habitual among animals. The power of the Press in promoting war is entirely due to the fact that it is able to appeal to certain instincts. Man is naturally competitive, acquisitive, and, in a greater or less degree, pugnacious. When the Press tells him that so-and-so is his enemy, a whole set of instincts in him responds to the suggestion. It is natural to most men to suppose that they have enemies and to find a certain fulfilment of their nature when they embark upon a contest. What a man believes upon grossly insufficient evidence is an index to his desires—desires of which he himself is often unconscious. If a man is offered a fact which goes against his instincts, he will scrutinize it closely, and unless the evidence is overwhelming, he will refuse to believe it. If, on the other hand, he is offered something which affords a reason for acting in accordance with his instincts, he will accept it even on the slenderest evidence. The origin of myths is explained in this way, and much of what is currently believed in international affairs is no better than myth. Although capitalism affords in modern society the channel by which the instinct of pugnacity finds its outlet, there is reason to fear that, if this channel were closed, some other would be found, unless education and environment were so changed as enormously to diminish the strength of the competitive instinct. If an economic reorganization can effect this it may provide a real safeguard against war, but if not, it is to be feared that the hopes of universal peace will prove delusive.

The abolition of capitalism might, and very likely would, greatly diminish the incentives to war which are derived from the Press and from the desire of finance to find new fields for investment in undeveloped countries, but those which are derived from the instinct of command and the impatience of opposition might remain, though perhaps in a less virulent form than at present. A democracy which has power is almost always more bellicose than one which is excluded from its due share in the government. The internationalism of Marx is based upon the assumption that the proletariat everywhere are oppressed by the ruling classes. The last words of the Communist Manifesto embody this idea:—

Let the ruling classes tremble at a Communistic revolution. The proletarians have nothing to lose but their chains. They have a world to win. Working men of all countries, unite!

So long as the proletarians have nothing to lose but their chains, it is not likely that their enmity will be directed against other proletarians. If the world had developed as Marx expected, the kind of internationalism which he foresaw might have inspired a universal social revolution. [Russia, which developed more nearly than any other country upon the lines of his system, has had a revolution of the kind which he expected.] If the development in other countries had been similar, it is highly probable that this revolution would have spread throughout the civilized world. The proletariat of all countries might have united against the capitalists as their common enemy, and in the bond of an identical hatred they might for the moment have been free from hatred toward each other. Even then, this ground of union would have ceased with their victory, and on the morrow of the social revolution the old national rivalries might have revived. There is no alchemy by which a universal harmony can be produced out of hatred. Those who have been inspired to action by the doctrine of the class war will have acquired the habit of hatred, and will instinctively seek new enemies when the old ones have been vanquished.

But in actual fact the psychology of the working man in any of the Western democracies is totally unlike that which is assumed in the Communist Manifesto. He does not by any means feel that he has nothing to lose but his chains, nor indeed is this true. The chains which bind Asia and Africa in subjection to Europe are partly riveted by him. He is himself part of a great system of tyranny and exploitation. Universal freedom would remove, not only his own chains, which are comparatively light, but the far heavier chains which he has helped to fasten upon the subject races of the world.

Not only do the working men of a country like England have a share in the benefit accruing from the exploitation of inferior races, but many among them also have their part in the capitalist system. The funds of Trade Unions and Friendly Societies are invested in ordinary undertakings, such as railways; many of the better-paid wage-earners have put their savings into government securities; and almost all who are politically active feel themselves part of the forces that determine public policy, through the power of the Labor Party and the greater unions. Owing to these causes their outlook on life has become to a considerable extent impregnated with capitalism and as their sense of power has grown, their nationalism has increased. This must continue to be true of any internationalism which is based upon hatred of the capitalist and adherence to the doctrine of the class war. Something more positive and constructive than this is needed if governing democracies are not to inherit the vices of governing classes in the past.

I do not wish to be thought to deny that capitalism does very much to promote wars, or that wars would probably be less frequent and less destructive if private property were abolished. On the contrary, I believe that the abolition of private ownership of land and capital is a necessary step toward any world in which the nations are to live at peace with one another. I am only arguing that this step, necessary as it is, will not alone suffice for this end, but that among the causes of war there are others that go deeper into the roots of human nature than any that orthodox Socialists are wont to acknowledge.

Let us take an instance. In Australia and California there is an intense dislike and fear toward the yellow races. The causes of this are complex; the chief among them are two, labor competition and instinctive race-hatred. It is probable that, if race-hatred did not exist, the difficulties of labor competition could be overcome. European immigrants also compete, but they are not excluded. In a sparsely populated country, industrious cheap labor could, with a little care, be so utilized as to enrich the existing inhabitants; it might, for example, be confined to certain kinds of work, by custom if not by law. But race-hatred opens men's minds to the evils of competition and closes them against the advantages of co-operation; it makes them regard with horror the somewhat unfamiliar vices of the aliens, while our own vices are viewed with mild toleration. I cannot but think that, if Australia were completely socialized, there would still remain the same popular objection as at present to any large influx of Chinese or Japanese labor. Yet if Japan also were to become a

Socialist State, the Japanese might well continue to feel the pressure of population and the desire for an outlet. In such circumstances, all the passions and interests required to produce a war would exist, in spite of the establishment of Socialism in both countries. Ants are as completely Socialistic as any community can possibly be, yet they put to death any ant which strays among them by mistake from a neighboring ant-heap. Men do not differ much from ants, as regards their instincts in this respect, wherever there is a great divergence of race, as between white men and yellow men. Of course the instinct of race-hostility can be overcome by suitable circumstances; but in the absence of such circumstances it remains a formidable menace to the world's peace.

If the peace of the world is ever to become secure, I believe there will have to be, along with other changes, a development of the idea which inspires the project of a League of Nations. As time goes on, the destructiveness of war grows greater and its profits grow less: the rational argument against war acquires more and more force as the increasing productivity of labor makes it possible to devote a greater and greater proportion of the population to the work of mutual slaughter. In quiet times, or when a great war has just ended, men's moods are amenable to the rational grounds in favor of peace, and it is possible to inaugurate schemes designed to make wars

INTERNATIONAL RELATIONS 153

less frequent. Probably no civilized nation would embark upon an aggressive war if it were fairly certain in advance that the aggressor must be defeated. This could be achieved if most great nations came to regard the peace of the world as of such importance that they would side against an aggressor even in a quarrel in which they had no direct interest. It is on this hope that the League of Nations is based.

But the League of Nations, like the abolition of private property, will be by no means sufficient if it is not accompanied or quickly followed by other reforms. It is clear that such reforms, if they are to be effective, must be international; the world must move as a whole in these matters, if it is to move at all. One of the most obvious necessities, if peace is to be secure, is a measure of disarmament. So long as the present vast armies and navies exist, no system can prevent the risk of war. But disarmament, if it is to serve its purpose, must be simultaneous and by mutual agreement among all the Great Powers. And it is not likely to be successful so long as hatred and suspicion rule between nations, for each nation will suspect its neighbor of not carrying out the bargain fairly. A different mental and moral atmosphere from that to which we are accustomed in international affairs will be necessary if agreements between nations are to succeed in averting catastrophes. If once such an atmosphere existed it might be perpetuated and strengthened by wise institutions; but it cannot be *created* by institutions alone. International co-operation requires mutual good will, and good will, however it has arisen, is only to be *preserved* by co-operation. The international future depends upon the possibility of the initial creation of good will between nations.

It is in this sort of matter that revolutions are most useful. If the Russian Revolution had been accompanied by a revolution in Germany, the dramatic suddenness of the change might have shaken Europe, for the moment, out of its habits of thought: the idea of fraternity might have seemed, in the twinkling of an eye, to have entered the world of practical politics; and no idea is so practical as the idea of the brotherhood of man, if only people can be startled into believing in it. If once the idea of fraternity between nations were inaugurated with the faith and vigor belonging to a new revolution, all the difficulties surrounding it would melt away, for all of them are due to suspicion and the tyranny of ancient prejudice. Those who (as is common in the English-speaking world) reject revolution as a method, and praise the gradual piecemeal development which (we are told) constitutes solid progress, overlook the effect of dramatic events in changing the mood and the beliefs of whole populations. A simultaneous revolution in Germany and Russia would no doubt have had such an effect, and would

INTERNATIONAL RELATIONS 155

have made the creation of a new world possible here and now.

Dis aliter visum: the millennium is not for our time. The great moment has passed, and for ourselves it is again the distant hope that must inspire us, not the immediate breathless looking for the deliverance.[1] But we have seen what *might* have been, and we know that great possibilities do arise in times of crisis. In some such sense as this, it may well be true that the Socialist revolution is the road to universal peace, and that when it has been traversed all the other conditions for the cessation of wars will grow of themselves out of the changed mental and moral atmosphere.

There is a certain class of difficulties which surrounds the sober idealist in all speculations about the not too distant future. These are the cases where the solution believed by most idealists to be universally applicable is for some reason impossible, and is, at the same time, objected to for base or interested motives by all upholders of existing inequalities. The case of Tropical Africa will illustrate what I mean. It would be difficult seriously to advocate the immediate introduction of parliamentary government for the natives of this part of the world, even if it were accompanied by women's suffrage and proportional

---

[1] This was written in March, 1918, almost the darkest moment of the war.

representation. So far as I know, no one supposes the populations of these regions capable of self-determination, except Mr. Lloyd George. There can be no doubt that, whatever *régime* may be introduced in Europe, African negroes will for a long time to come be governed and exploited by Europeans. If the European States became Socialistic, and refused, under a Quixotic impulse, to enrich themselves at the expense of the defenseless inhabitants of Africa, those inhabitants would not thereby gain; on the contrary, they would lose, for they would be handed over to the tender mercies of individual traders, operating with armies of reprobate bravos, and committing every atrocity to which the civilized barbarian is prone. The European governments cannot divest themselves of responsibility in regard to Africa. They must govern there, and the best that can be hoped is that they should govern with a minimum of cruelty and rapacity. From the point of view of preserving the peace of the world, the problem is to parcel out the advantages which white men derive from their position in Africa in such a way that no nation shall feel a sense of injustice. This problem is comparatively simple, and might no doubt be solved on the lines of the war aims of the Inter-Allied Socialists. But it is not this problem which I wish to discuss. What I wish to consider is, how could a Socialist or an Anarchist community govern and administer an African region, full of natural wealth, but inhabited by a quite uncivilized population? Unless great precautions were taken the white community, under the circumstances, would acquire the position and the instincts of a slave-owner. It would tend to keep the negroes down to the bare level of subsistence, while using the produce of their country to increase the comfort and splendor of the Communist community. It would do this with that careful unconsciousness which now characterizes all the worst acts of nations. Administrators would be appointed and would be expected to keep silence as to their methods. Busybodies who reported horrors would be disbelieved, and would be said to be actuated by hatred toward the existing *régime* and by a perverse love for every country but their own. No doubt, in the first generous enthusiasm accompanying the establishment of the new *régime* at home, there would be every intention of making the natives happy, but gradually they would be forgotten, and only the tribute coming from their country would be remembered. I do not say that all these evils are unavoidable; I say only that they will not be avoided unless they are foreseen and a deliberate conscious effort is made to prevent their realization. If the white communities should ever reach the point of wishing to carry out as far as possible the principles underlying the revolt against capitalism, they will have to find a way of establishing an absolute disinterestedness in their dealings with subject races. It will be necessary to avoid the faintest suggestion of capitalistic profit in the government of Africa, and to spend in the countries themselves whatever they would be able to spend if they were self-governing. Moreover, it must always be remembered that backwardness in civilization is not necessarily incurable, and that with time even the populations of Central Africa may become capable of democratic self-government, provided Europeans bend their energies to this purpose.

The problem of Africa is, of course, a part of the wider problems of Imperialism, but it is that part in which the application of Socialist principles is most difficult. In regard to Asia, and more particularly in regard to India and Persia, the application of principles is clear in theory though difficult in political practice. The obstacles to self-government which exist in Africa do not exist in the same measure in Asia. What stands in the way of freedom of Asiatic populations is not their lack of intelligence, but only their lack of military prowess, which makes them an easy prey to our lust for dominion. This lust would probably be in temporary abeyance on the morrow of a Socialist revolution, and at such a moment a new departure in Asiatic policy might be taken with permanently beneficial results. I do not mean, of

course, that we should force upon India that form
of democratic government which we have developed
for our own needs. I mean rather that we should
leave India to choose its own form of government, its
own manner of education and its own type of civilization. India has an ancient tradition, very different
from that of Western Europe, a tradition highly
valued by educated Hindoos, but not loved by our
schools and colleges. The Hindoo Nationalist feels
that his country has a type of culture containing elements of value that are absent, or much less marked,
in the West; he wishes to be free to preserve this,
and desires political freedom for such reasons rather
than for those that would most naturally appeal to
an Englishman in the same subject position. The
belief of the European in his own Kultur tends to be
fanatical and ruthless, and for this reason, as much as
for any other, the independence of extra-European
civilization is of real importance to the world, for it is
not by a dead uniformity that the world as a whole is
most enriched.

I have set forth strongly all the major difficulties
in the way of the preservation of the world's peace,
not because I believe these difficulties to be insuperable, but, on the contrary, because I believe that they
can be overcome if they are recognized. A correct
diagnosis is necessarily the first step toward a cure.
The existing evils in international relations spring,

at bottom, from psychological causes, from motives forming part of human nature as it is at present. Among these the chief are competitiveness, love of power, and envy, using envy in that broad sense in which it includes the instinctive dislike of any gain to others not accompanied by an at least equal gain to ourselves. The evils arising from these three causes can be removed by a better education and a better economic and political system.

Competitiveness is by no means wholly an evil. When it takes the form of emulation in the service of the public, or in discovery or the production of works of art, it may become a very useful stimulus, urging men to profitable effort beyond what they would otherwise make. It is only harmful when it aims at the acquisition of goods which are limited in amount, so that what one man possesses he holds at the expense of another. When competitiveness takes this form it is necessarily attended by fear, and out of fear cruelty is almost inevitably developed. But a social system providing for a more just distribution of material goods might close to the instinct of competitiveness those channels in which it is harmful, and cause it to flow instead in channels in which it would become a benefit to mankind. This is one great reason why the communal ownership of land and capital would be likely to have a beneficial effect upon human nature, for human nature, as it exists in adult men and women, is by no means a fixed datum, but a product of circumstances, education and opportunity operating upon a highly malleable native disposition.

What is true of competitiveness is equally true of love of power. Power, in the form in which it is now usually sought, is power of command, power of imposing one's will upon others by force, open or concealed. This form of power consists, in essence, in thwarting others, for it is only displayed when others are compelled to do what they do not wish to do. Such power, we hope, the social system which is to supersede capitalism will reduce to a minimum by the methods which we outlined in the preceding chapter. These methods can be applied in international no less than in national affairs. In international affairs the same formula of federalism will apply: self-determination for every group in regard to matters which concern it much more vitally than they concern others, and government by a neutral authority embracing rival groups in all matters in which conflicting interests of groups come into play; but always with the fixed principle that the functions of government are to be reduced to the bare minimum compatible with justice and the prevention of private violence. In such a world the present harmful outlets for the love of power would be closed. But the power which consists in persuasion, in teaching, in leading men to a new wisdom or the realization of new possibilities of happiness—this kind of power, which may be wholly beneficial, would remain untouched, and many vigorous men, who in the actual world devote their energies to domination, would in such a world find their energies directed to the creation of new goods rather than the perpetuation of ancient evils.

Envy, the third of the psychological causes to which we attributed what is bad in the actual world, depends in most natures upon that kind of fundamental discontent which springs from a lack of free development, from thwarted instinct, and from the impossibility of realizing an imagined happiness. Envy cannot be cured by preaching; preaching, at the best, will only alter its manifestations and lead it to adopt more subtle forms of concealment. Except in those rare natures in which generosity dominates in spite of circumstances, the only cure for envy is freedom and the joy of life. From populations largely deprived of the simple instinctive pleasures of leisure and love, sunshine and green fields, generosity of outlook and kindliness of dispositions are hardly to be expected. In such populations these qualities are not likely to be found, even among the fortunate few, for these few are aware, however dimly, that they are profiting by an injustice, and that they can only continue to enjoy their good fortune by deliberately ignoring those with whom it is not shared. If generosity and kindliness are to be common, there must be more care than there is at present for the elementary wants of human nature, and more realization that the diffusion of happiness among all who are not the victims of some peculiar misfortune is both possible and imperative. A world full of happiness would not wish to plunge into war, and would not be filled with that grudging hostility which our cramped and narrow existence forces upon average human nature. A world full of happiness is not beyond human power to create; the obstacles imposed by inanimate nature are not insuperable. The real obstacles lie in the heart of man, and the cure for these is a firm hope, informed and fortified by thought.

CHAPTER VII

SCIENCE AND ART UNDER SOCIALISM

SOCIALISM has been advocated by most of its champions chiefly as a means of increasing the welfare of the wage-earning classes, and more particularly their material welfare. It has seemed accordingly, to some men whose aims are not material, as if it has nothing to offer toward the general advancement of civilization in the way of art and thought. Some of its advocates, moreover—and among these Marx must be included—have written, no doubt not deliberately, as if with the Socialist revolution the millennium would have arrived, and there would be no need of further progress for the human race. I do not know whether our age is more restless than that which preceded it, or whether it has merely become more impregnated with the idea of evolution, but, for whatever reason, we have grown incapable of believing in a state of static perfection, and we demand, of any social system, which is to have our approval, that it shall contain within itself a stimulus and opportunity for progress toward something still bettter. The doubts thus raised by Socialist writers make it necessary to inquire whether Socialism would in fact be hostile to art and science, and whether it would be likely to produce a stereotyped society in which progress would become difficult and slow.

It is not enough that men and women should be made comfortable in a material sense. Many members of the well-to-do classes at present, in spite of opportunity, contribute nothing of value to the life of the world, and do not even succeed in securing for themselves any personal happiness worthy to be so called. The multiplication of such individuals would be an achievement of the very minutest value; and if Socialism were merely to bestow upon all the kind of life and outlook which is now enjoyed by the more apathetic among the well-to-do, it would offer little that could inspire enthusiasm in any generous spirit.

"The true rôle of collective existence," says M. Naquet,[1] " . . . is to learn, to discover, to know. Eating, drinking, sleeping, living, in a word, is a mere accessory. In this respect, we are not distinguished from the brute. Knowledge is the goal. If I were condemned to choose between a humanity materially happy, glutted after the manner of a flock of sheep in a field, and a humanity existing in misery, but from which emanated, here and there, some eternal truth, it is on the latter that my choice would fall."

---

[1] "L'Anarchie et le Collectivisme," p. 114.

This statement puts the alternative in a very extreme form in which it is somewhat unreal. It may be said in reply that for those who have had the leisure and the opportunity to enjoy " eternal truths " it is easy to exalt their importance at the expense of sufferings which fall on others. This is true; but, if it is taken as disposing of the question, it leaves out of account the importance of thought for progress. Viewing the life of mankind as a whole, in the future as well as in the present, there can be no question that a society in which some men pursue knowledge while others endure great poverty offers more hope of ultimate good than a society in which all are sunk in slothful comfort. It is true that poverty is a great evil, but it is not true that material prosperity is in itself a great good. If it is to have any real value to society, it must be made a means to the advancement of those higher goods that belong to the life of the mind. But the life of the mind does not consist of thought and knowledge alone, nor can it be completely healthy unless it has some instinctive contact, however deeply buried, with the general life of the community. Divorced from the social instinct, thought, like art, tends to become finicky and precious. It is the position of such art and thought as is imbued with the instinctive sense of service to mankind that we wish to consider, for it is this alone that makes up the life of the mind in the sense in which it is a vital part of the life of the community. Will the life of the mind in this sense be helped or hindered by Socialism? And will there still be a sufficient spur to progress to prevent a condition of Byzantine immobility?

In considering this question we are, in a certain sense, passing outside the atmosphere of democracy. The general good of the community is realized only in individuals, but it is realized much more fully in some individuals than in others. Some men have a comprehensive and penetrating intellect, enabling them to appreciate and remember what has been thought and known by their predecessors, and to discover new regions in which they enjoy all the high delights of the mental explorer. Others have the power of creating beauty, giving bodily form to impalpable visions out of which joy comes to many. Such men are more fortunate than the mass, and also more important for the collective life. A larger share of the general sum of good is concentrated in them than in the ordinary man and woman; but also their contribution to the general good is greater. They stand out among men and cannot be wholly fitted into the framework of democratic equality. A social system which would render them unproductive would stand condemned, whatever other merits it might have.

The first thing to realize—though it is difficult in

a commercial age—is that what is best in creative mental activity cannot be produced by any system of monetary rewards. Opportunity and the stimulus of an invigorating spiritual atmosphere are important, but, if they are presented, no financial inducements will be required, while if they are absent, material compensations will be of no avail. Recognition, even if it takes the form of money, can bring a certain pleasure in old age to the man of science who has battled all his life against academic prejudice, or to the artist who has endured years of ridicule for not painting in the manner of his predecessors; but it is not by the remote hope of such pleasures that their work has been inspired. All the most important work springs from an uncalculating impulse, and is best promoted, not by rewards after the event, but by circumstances which keep the impulse alive and afford scope for the activities which it inspires. In the creation of such circumstances our present system is much at fault. Will Socialism be better?

I do not think this question can be answered without specifying the kind of Socialism that is intended: some forms of Socialism would, I believe, be even more destructive in this respect than the present capitalist *régime*, while others would be immeasurably better. Three things which a social system can provide or withhold are helpful to mental creation:

first, technical training; second, liberty to follow the creative impulse; third, at least the possibility of ultimate appreciation by some public, whether large or small. We may leave out of our discussion both individual genius and those intangible conditions which make some ages great and others sterile in art and science—not because these are unimportant, but because they are too little understood to be taken account of in economic or political organization. The three conditions we have mentioned seem to cover most of what can be *seen* to be useful or harmful from our present point of view, and it is therefore to them that we shall confine ourselves.

1. *Technical Training.*—Technical training at present, whether in science or art, requires one or other of two conditions. Either a boy must be the son of well-to-do parents who can afford to keep him while he acquires his education, or he must show so much ability at an early age as to enable him to subsist on scholarships until he is ready to earn his living. The former condition is, of course, a mere matter of luck, and could not be preserved in its present form under any kind of Socialism or Communism. This loss is emphasized by defenders of the present system, and no doubt it would be, to some extent, a real loss. But the well-to-do are a small proportion of the population, and presumably on the average no more talented by nature than their less

fortunate contemporaries. If the advantages which are enjoyed now by those few among them who are capable of good work in science or art could be extended, even in a slightly attenuated form, to all who are similarly gifted, the result would almost infallibly be a gain, and much ability which is now wasted would be rendered fruitful. But how is this to be effected?

The system of scholarships obtained by competition, though better than nothing, is objectionable from many points of view. It introduces the competitive spirit into the work of the very young; it makes them regard knowledge from the standpoint of what is useful in examinations rather than in the light of its intrinsic interest or importance; it places a premium upon that sort of ability which is displayed precociously in glib answers to set questions rather than upon the kind that broods on difficulties and remains for a time rather dumb. What is perhaps worse than any of these defects is the tendency to cause overwork in youth, leading to lack of vigor and interest when manhood has been reached. It can hardly be doubted that by this cause, at present, many fine minds have their edge blunted and their keenness destroyed.

State Socialism might easily universalize the system of scholarships obtained by competitive examination, and if it did so it is to be feared that it would be very harmful. State Socialists at present tend to be enamored of the system, which is exactly of the kind that every bureaucrat loves: orderly, neat, giving a stimulus to industrious habits, and involving no waste of a sort that could be tabulated in statistics or accounts of public expenditure. Such men will argue that free higher education is expensive to the community, and only useful in the case of those who have exceptional abilities; it ought, therefore, they will say, not to be given to all, but only to those who will become more useful members of society through receiving it. Such arguments make a great appeal to what are called " practical " men, and the answers to them are of a sort which it is difficult to render widely convincing. Revolt against the evils of competition is, however, part of the very essence of the Socialist's protest against the existing order, and on this ground, if on no other, those who favor Socialism may be summoned to look for some better solution.

Much the simplest solution, and the only really effective one, is to make every kind of education free up to the age of twenty-one for all boys and girls who desire it. The majority will be tired of education before that age, and will prefer to begin other work sooner; this will lead to a natural selection of those with strong interests in some pursuit requiring a long training. Among those selected in this way

by their own inclinations, probably almost all who
have marked abilities of the kind in question will be
included. It is true that there will also be many
who have very little ability; the desire to become a
painter, for example, is by no means confined to
those who can paint. But this degree of waste could
well be borne by the community; it would be immeasurably less than that now entailed by the support of the idle rich. Any system which aims at
avoiding this kind of waste must entail the far more
serious waste of rejecting or spoiling some of the
best ability in each generation. The system of free
education up to any grade for all who desire it is
the only system which is consistent with the principles
of liberty, and the only one which gives a reasonable
hope of affording full scope for talent. This system
is equally compatible with all forms of Socialism
and Anarchism. Theoretically, it is compatible with
capitalism, but practically it is so opposite in spirit
that it would hardly be feasible without a complete
economic reconstruction. The fact that Socialism
would facilitate it must be reckoned a very powerful
argument in favor of change, for the waste of talent
at present in the poorer classes of society must be
stupendous.

2. *Liberty to follow the creative impulse.*—
When a man's training has been completed, if he is
possessed of really great abilities, he will do his best

SCIENCE AND ART UNDER SOCIALISM

work if he is completely free to follow his bent, creating what seems good to him, regardless of the judgment of "experts." At present this is only possible for two classes of people: those who have private means, and those who can earn a living by an occupation that does not absorb their whole energies. Under Socialism, there will be no one with private means, and if there is to be no loss as regards art and science, the opportunity which now comes by accident to a few will have to be provided deliberately for a much larger number. The men who have used private means as an opportunity for creative work have been few but important: one might mention Milton, Shelley, Keats and Darwin as examples. Probably none of these would have produced as good work if they had had to earn their livelihood. If Darwin had been a university teacher, he would of course have been dismissed from his post by the influence of the clerics on account of his scandalous theories.

Nevertheless, the bulk of the creative work of the world is done at present by men who subsist by some other occupation. Science, and research generally, are usually done in their spare time by men who live by teaching. There is no great objection to this in the case of science, provided the number of hours devoted to teaching is not excessive. It is partly because science and teaching are so easily combined that science is vigorous in the present age. In music, a composer who is also a performer enjoys similar advantages, but one who is not a performer must starve, unless he is rich or willing to pander to the public taste. In the fine arts, as a rule, it is not easy in the modern world either to make a living by really good work or to find a subsidiary profession which leaves enough leisure for creation. This is presumably one reason, though by no means the only one, why art is less flourishing than science.

The bureaucratic State Socialist will have a simple solution for these difficulties. He will appoint a body consisting of the most eminent celebrities in an art or a science, whose business it shall be to judge the work of young men, and to issue licenses to those whose productions find favor in their eyes. A licensed artist shall be considered to have performed his duty to the community by producing works of art. But of course he will have to prove his industry by never failing to produce in reasonable quantities, and his continued ability by never failing to please his eminent judges—until, in the fulness of time, he becomes a judge himself. In this way, the authorities will insure that the artist shall be competent, regular, and obedient to the best traditions of his art. Those who fail to fulfil these conditions will be compelled by the withdrawal of their license to seek some less dubious mode of earning their living. Such will be the ideal of the State Socialist.

In such a world all that makes life tolerable to the lover of beauty would perish. Art springs from a wild and anarchic side of human nature; between the artist and the bureaucrat there must always be a profound mutual antagonism, an age-long battle in which the artist, always outwardly worsted, wins in the end through the gratitude of mankind for the joy that he puts into their lives. If the wild side of human nature is to be permanently subjected to the orderly rules of the benevolent, uncomprehending bureaucrat, the joy of life will perish out of the earth, and the very impulse to live will gradually wither and die. Better a thousandfold the present world with all its horrors than such a dead mummy of a world. Better Anarchism, with all its risks, than a State Socialism that subjects to rule what must be spontaneous and free if it is to have any value. It is this nightmare that makes artists, and lovers of beauty generally, so often suspicious of Socialism. But there is nothing in the essence of Socialism to make art impossible: only certain forms of Socialism would entail this danger. William Morris was a Socialist, and was a Socialist very largely because he was an artist. And in this he was not irrational.

It is impossible for art, or any of the higher

creative activities, to flourish under any system which requires that the artist shall prove his competence to some body of authorities before he is allowed to follow his impulse. Any really great artist is almost sure to be thought incompetent by those among his seniors who would be generally regarded as best qualified to form an opinion. And the mere fact of having to produce work which will please older men is hostile to a free spirit and to bold innovation. Apart from this difficulty, selection by older men would lead to jealousy and intrigue and back-biting, producing a poisonous atmosphere of underground competition. The only effect of such a plan would be to eliminate the few who now slip through owing to some fortunate accident. It is not by any system, but by freedom alone, that art can flourish.

There are two ways by which the artist could secure freedom under Socialism of the right kind. He might undertake regular work outside his art, doing only a few hours' work a day and receiving proportionately less pay than those who do a full day's work. He ought, in that case, to be at liberty to sell his pictures if he could find purchasers. Such a system would have many advantages. It would leave absolutely every man free to become an artist, provided he were willing to suffer a certain economic loss. This would not deter those in whom the impulse was strong and genuine, but would tend to

SCIENCE AND ART UNDER SOCIALISM 177

exclude the dilettante. Many young artists at present endure voluntarily much greater poverty than need be entailed by only doing half the usual day's work in a well-organized Socialist community; and some degree of hardship is not objectionable, as a test of the strength of the creative impulse, and as an offset to the peculiar joys of the creative life.

The other possibility [1] would be that the necessaries of life should be free, as Anarchists desire, to all equally, regardless of whether they work or not. Under this plan, every man could live without work: there would be what might be called a "vagabond's wage," sufficient for existence but not for luxury. The artist who preferred to have his whole time for art and enjoyment might live on the "vagabond's wage"—traveling on foot when the humor seized him to see foreign countries, enjoying the air and the sun, as free as the birds, and perhaps scarcely less happy. Such men would bring color and diversity into the life of the community; their outlook would be different from that of steady, stay-at-home workers, and would keep alive a much-needed element of light-heartedness which our sober, serious civilization tends to kill. If they became very numerous, they might be too great an economic burden on the workers; but I doubt if there are many with enough capacity for simple enjoyments to choose poverty and free-

---
[1] Which we discussed in Chapter IV.

dom in preference to the comparatively light and pleasant work which will be usual in those days.

By either of these methods, freedom can be preserved for the artist in a socialistic commonwealth—far more complete freedom, and far more widespread, than any that now exists except for the possessors of capital.

But there still remain some not altogether easy problems. Take, for example, the publishing of books. There will not, under Socialism, be private publishers as at present: under State Socialism, presumably the State will be the sole publisher, while under Syndicalism or Guild Socialism the *Fédération du Livre* will have the whole of the trade in its hands. Under these circumstances, who is to decide what MSS. are to be printed? It is clear that opportunities exist for an Index more rigorous than that of the Inquisition. If the State were the sole publisher, it would doubtless refuse books opposed to State Socialism. If the *Fédération du Livre* were the ultimate arbiter, what publicity could be obtained for works criticising it? And apart from such political difficulties we should have, as regards literature, that very censorship by eminent officials which we agreed to regard as disastrous when we were considering the fine arts in general. The difficulty is serious, and a way of meeting it must be found if literature is to remain free.

Kropotkin, who believes that manual and intellectual work should be combined, holds that authors themselves should be compositors, bookbinders, etc. He even seems to suggest that the whole of the manual work involved in producing books should be done by authors. It may be doubted whether there are enough authors in the world for this to be possible, and in any case I cannot but think that it would be a waste of time for them to leave the work they understand in order to do badly work which others could do far better and more quickly. That, however, does not touch our present point, which is the question how the MSS. to be printed will be selected. In Kropotkin's plan there will presumably be an Author's Guild, with a Committee of Management, if Anarchism allows such things. . This Committee of Management will decide which of the books submitted to it are worthy to be printed. Among these will be included those by the Committee and their friends, but not those by their enemies. Authors of rejected MSS. will hardly have the patience to spend their time setting up the works of successful rivals, and there will have to be an elaborate system of log-rolling if any books are to be printed at all. It hardly looks as if this plan would conduce to harmony among literary men, or would lead to the publication of any book of an unconventional tendency.

Kropotkin's own books, for example, would hardly have found favor.

The only way of meeting these difficulties, whether under State Socialism or Guild Socialism or Anarchism, seems to be by making it possible for an author to pay for the publication of his book if it is not such as the State or the Guild is willing to print at its own expense. I am aware that this method is contrary to the spirit of Socialism, but I do not see what other way there is of securing freedom. The payment might be made by undertaking to engage for an assigned period in some work of recognized utility and to hand over such proportion of the earnings as might be necessary. The work undertaken might of course be, as Kropotkin suggests, the manual part of the production of books, but I see no special reason why it should be. It would have to be an absolute rule that no book should be refused, no matter what the nature of its contents might be, if payment for publication were offered at the standard rate. An author who had admirers would be able to secure their help in payment. An unknown author might, it is true, have to suffer a considerable loss of comfort in order to make his payment, but that would give an automatic means of eliminating those whose writing was not the result of any very profound impulse and would be by no means wholly an evil.

Probably some similar method would be desirable

as regards the publishing and performing of new music.

What we have been suggesting will, no doubt, be objected to by orthodox Socialists, since they will find something repugnant to their principles in the whole idea of a private person paying to have certain work done. But it is a mistake to be the slave of a system, and every system, if it is applied rigidly, will entail evils which could only be avoided by some concession to the exigencies of special cases. On the whole, a wise form of Socialism might afford infinitely better opportunities for the artist and the man of science than are possible in a capitalist community; but only if the form of Socialism adopted is one which is fitted for this end by means of provisions such as we have been suggesting.

3. *Possibility of Appreciation.*—This condition is one which is not necessary to all who do creative work, but in the sense in which I mean it the great majority find it very nearly indispensable. I do not mean widespread public recognition, nor that ignorant, half-sincere respect which is commonly accorded to artists who have achieved success. Neither of these serves much purpose. What I mean is rather understanding, and a spontaneous feeling that things of beauty are important. In a thoroughly commercialized society, an artist is repected if he makes money, and because he makes money, but there is no

genuine respect for the works of art by which his money has been made. A millionaire whose fortune has been made in button-hooks or chewing-gum is regarded with awe, but none of this feeling is bestowed on the articles from which his wealth is derived. In a society which measures all things by money the same tends to be true of the artist. If he has become rich he is respected, though of course less than the millionaire, but his pictures or books or music are regarded as the chewing-gum or the button-hooks are regarded, merely as a means to money. In such an atmosphere it is very difficult for the artist to preserve his creative impulse pure: either he is contaminated by his surroundings, or he becomes embittered through lack of appreciation for the object of his endeavor.

It is not appreciation of the artist that is necessary so much as appreciation of the art. It is difficult for an artist to live in an environment in which everything is judged by its utility, rather than by its intrinsic quality. The whole side of life of which art is the flower requires something which may be called disinterestedness, a capacity for direct enjoyment without thought of tomorrow's problems and difficulties. When people are amused by a joke they do not need to be persuaded that it will serve some important purpose. The same kind of direct pleasure is involved in any genuine appreciation of art.

The struggle for life, the serious work of a trade or profession, is apt to make people too solemn for jokes and too pre-occupied for art. The easing of the struggle, the diminution in the hours of work, and the lightening of the burden of existence, which would result from a better economic system, could hardly fail to increase the joy of life and the vital energy available for sheer delight in the world. And if this were achieved there would inevitably be more spontaneous pleasure in beautiful things, and more enjoyment of the work of artists. But none of these good results are to be expected from the mere removal of poverty: they all require also a diffused sense of freedom, and the absence of that feeling of oppression by a vast machine which now weighs down the individual spirit. I do not think State Socialism can give this sense of freedom, but some other forms of Socialism, which have absorbed what is true in Anarchist teaching, can give it to a degree of which capitalism is wholly incapable.

A general sense of progress and achievement is an immense stimulus to all forms of creative work. For this reason, a great deal will depend, not only in material ways, upon the question whether methods of production in industry and agriculture become stereotyped or continue to change rapidly as they have done during the last hundred years. Improved methods of production will be much more obviously than now to the interest of the community at large, when what every man receives is his due share of the total produce of labor. But there will probably not be any individuals with the same direct and intense interest in technical improvements as now belongs to the capitalist in manufacture. If the natural conservatism of the workers is not to prove stronger than their interest in increasing production, it will be necessary that, when better methods are introduced by the workers in any industry, part at least of the benefit should be allowed for a time to be retained by them. If this is done, it may be presumed that each Guild will be continually seeking for new processes or inventions, and will value those technical parts of scientific research which are useful for this purpose. With every improvement, the question will arise whether it is to be used to give more leisure or to increase the dividend of commodities. Where there is so much more leisure than there is now, there will be many more people with a knowledge of science or an understanding of art. The artist or scientific investigator will be far less cut off than he is at present from the average citizen, and this will almost inevitably be a stimulus to his creative energy.

I think we may fairly conclude that, from the point of view of all three requisites for art and science, namely, training, freedom and appreciation, State Socialism would largely fail to remove existing

SCIENCE AND ART UNDER SOCIALISM 185

evils and would introduce new evils of its own; but Guild Socialism, or even Syndicalism, if it adopted a liberal policy toward those who preferred to work less than the usual number of hours at recognized occupations, might be immeasurably preferable to anything that is possible under the rule of capitalism. There are dangers, but they will all vanish if the importance of liberty is adequately acknowledged. In this as in nearly everything else, the road to all that is best is the road of freedom.

CHAPTER VIII

THE WORLD AS IT COULD BE MADE

In the daily lives of most men and women, fear plays a greater part than hope: they are more filled with the thought of the possessions that others may take from them, than of the joy that they might create in their own lives and in the lives with which they come in contact.

It is not so that life should be lived.

Those whose lives are fruitful to themselves, to their friends, or to the world are inspired by hope and sustained by joy: they see in imagination the things that might be and the way in which they are to be brought into existence. In their private relations they are not pre-occupied with anxiety lest they should lose such affection and respect as they receive: they are engaged in giving affection and respect freely, and the reward comes of itself without their seeking. In their work they are not haunted by jealousy of competitors, but concerned with the actual matter that has to be done. In politics, they do not spend time and passion defending unjust privileges of their class or nation, but they aim at making the world as a whole happier, less cruel, less full of conflict between rival greeds, and more full of human beings whose growth has not been dwarfed and stunted by oppression.

A life lived in this spirit— the spirit that aims at creating rather than possessing—has a certain fundamental happiness, of which it cannot be wholly robbed by adverse circumstances. This is the way of life recommended in the Gospels, and by all the great teachers of the world. Those who have found it are freed from the tyranny of fear, since what they value most in their lives is not at the mercy of outside power. If all men could summon up the courage and the vision to live in this way in spite of obstacles and discouragement, there would be no need for the regeneration of the world to begin by political and economic reform: all that is needed in the way of reform would come automatically, without resistance, owing to the moral regeneration of individuals. But the teaching of Christ has been nominally accepted by the world for many centuries, and yet those who follow it are still persecuted as they were before the time of Constantine. Experience has proved that few are able to see through the apparent evils of an outcast's life to the inner joy that comes of faith and creative hope. If the domination of fear is to be overcome, it is not enough, as regards the mass of men, to preach courage and indifference to misfortune: it is necessary to remove the causes of fear, to make a good life no longer an unsuccessful one in a worldly sense, and to diminish the harm that can be inflicted upon those who are not wary in self-defense.

When we consider the evils in the lives we know of, we find that they may be roughly divided into three classes. There are, first, those due to physical nature: among these are death, pain and the difficulty of making the soil yield a subsistence. These we will call "physical evils." Second, we may put those that spring from defects in the character or aptitudes of the sufferer: among these are ignorance, lack of will, and violent passions. These we will call "evils of character." Third come those that depend upon the power of one individual or group over another: these comprise not only obvious tyranny, but all interference with free development, whether by force or by excessive mental influence such as may occur in education. These we will call "evils of power." A social system may be judged by its bearing upon these three kinds of evils.

The distinction between the three kinds cannot be sharply drawn. Purely physical evil is a limit, which we can never be sure of having reached: we cannot abolish death, but we can often postpone it by science, and it may ultimately become possible to secure that the great majority shall live till old age; we cannot wholly prevent pain, but we can diminish it indefinitely by securing a healthy life for all; we cannot make the earth yield its fruits in any abundance without labor, but we can diminish the amount of the labor and improve its conditions until it ceases to be an evil. Evils of character are often the result of physical evil in the shape of illness, and still more often the result of evils of power, since tyranny degrades both those who exercise it and (as a rule) those who suffer it. Evils of power are intensified by evils of character in those who have power, and by fear of the physical evil which is apt to be the lot of those who have no power. For all these reasons, the three sorts of evil are intertwined. Nevertheless, speaking broadly, we may distinguish among our misfortunes those which have their proximate cause in the material world, those which are mainly due to defects in ourselves, and those which spring from our being subject to the control of others.

The main methods of combating these evils are: for physical evils, science; for evils of character, education (in the widest sense) and a free outlet for all impulses that do not involve domination; for evils of power, the reform of the political and economic organization of society in such a way as to reduce to the lowest possible point the interference of one man with the life of another. We will begin with the third of these kinds of evil, because it is evils of power specially that Socialism and Anarchism have sought to remedy. Their protest against inequalities of wealth has rested mainly upon their sense of the evils arising from the power conferred by wealth. This point has been well stated by Mr. G. D. H. Cole:—

What, I want to ask, is the fundamental evil in our modern Society which we should set out to abolish?

There are two possible answers to that question, and I am sure that very many well-meaning people would make the wrong one. They would answer POVERTY, when they ought to answer SLAVERY. Face to face every day with the shameful contrasts of riches and destitution, high dividends and low wages, and painfully conscious of the futility of trying to adjust the balance by means of charity, private or public, they would answer unhesitatingly that they stand for the ABOLITION OF POVERTY.

Well and good! On that issue every Socialist is with them. But their answer to my question is none the less wrong.

Poverty is the symptom: slavery the disease. The extremes of riches and destitution follow inevitably upon the extremes of license and bondage. The many are not enslaved because they are poor, they are poor because they are enslaved. Yet Socialists have all too often fixed their eyes upon the material misery of the poor without realizing that it rests upon the spiritual degradation of the slave.[1]

---

[1] "Self-Government in Industry," G. Bell & Sons, 1917, pp. 110–111.

I do not think any reasonable person can doubt that the evils of power in the present system are vastly greater than is necessary, nor that they might be immeasurably diminished by a suitable form of Socialism. A few fortunate people, it is true, are now enabled to live freely on rent or interest, and they could hardly have more liberty under another system. But the great bulk, not only of the very poor, but of all sections of wage-earners and even of the professional classes, are the slaves of the need for getting money. Almost all are compelled to work so hard that they have little leisure for enjoyment or for pursuits outside their regular occupation. Those who are able to retire in later middle age are bored, because they have not learned how to fill their time when they are at liberty, and such interests as they once had apart from work have dried up. Yet these are the exceptionally fortunate: the majority have to work hard till old age, with the fear of destitution always before them, the richer ones dreading that they will be unable to give their children the education or the medical care that they consider desirable, the poorer ones often not far removed from starvation. And almost all who work have no voice in the direction of their work; throughout the hours of labor they are mere machines carrying out the will of a master. Work is usually done under disagreeable conditions, involving pain and physical hardship.

The only motive to work is wages: the very idea that work might be a joy, like the work of the artist, is usually scouted as utterly Utopian.

But by far the greater part of these evils are wholly unnecessary. If the civilized portion of mankind could be induced to desire their own happiness more than another's pain, if they could be induced to work constructively for improvements which they would share with all the world rather than destructively to prevent other classes or nations from stealing a march on them, the whole system by which the world's work is done might be reformed root and branch within a generation.

From the point of view of liberty, what system would be the best? In what direction should we wish the forces of progress to move?

From this point of view, neglecting for the moment all other considerations, I have no doubt that the best system would be one not far removed from that advocated by Kropotkin, but rendered more practicable by the adoption of the main principles of Guild Socialism. Since every point can be disputed, I will set down without argument the kind of organization of work that would seem best.

Education should be compulsory up to the age of 16, or perhaps longer; after that, it should be continued or not at the option of the pupil, but remain free (for those who desire it) up to at least the age of 21. When education is finished no one should be *compelled* to work, and those who choose not to work should receive a bare livelihood, and be left completely free; but probably it would be desirable that there should be a strong public opinion in favor of work, so that only comparatively few should choose idleness. One great advantage of making idleness economically possible is that it would afford a powerful motive for making work not disagreeable; and no community where most work is disagreeable can be said to have found a solution of economic problems. I think it is reasonable to assume that few would choose idleness, in view of the fact that even now at least nine out of ten of those who have (say) £100 a year from investments prefer to increase their income by paid work.

Coming now to that great majority who will not choose idleness, I think we may assume that, with the help of science, and by the elimination of the vast amount of unproductive work involved in internal and international competition, the whole community could be kept in comfort by means of four hours' work a day. It is already being urged by experienced employers that their employes can actually produce as much in a six-hour day as they can when they work eight hours. In a world where there is a much higher level of technical instruction than there is now the same tendency will be accentuated. People will be taught not only, as at present, one trade, or one small portion of a trade, but several trades, so that they can vary their occupation according to the seasons and the fluctuations of demand. Every industry will be self-governing as regards all its internal affairs, and even separate factories will decide for themselves all questions that only concern those who work in them. There will not be capitalist management, as at present, but management by elected representatives, as in politics. Relations between different groups of producers will be settled by the Guild Congress, matters concerning the community as the inhabitants of a certain area will continue to be decided by Parliament, while all disputes between Parliament and the Guild Congress will be decided by a body composed of representatives of both in equal numbers.

Payment will not be made, as at present, only for work actually required and performed, but for willingness to work. This system is already adopted in much of the better paid work: a man occupies a certain position, and retains it even at times when there happens to be very little to do. The dread of unemployment and loss of livelihood will no longer haunt men like a nightmare. Whether all who are willing to work will be paid equally, or whether exceptional skill will still command exceptional pay, is a matter which may be left to each guild to decide for itself.

An opera-singer who received no more pay than a scene-shifter might choose to be a scene-shifter until the system was changed: if so, higher pay would probably be found necessary. But if it were freely voted by the Guild, it could hardly constitute a grievance.

Whatever might be done toward making work agreeable, it is to be presumed that some trades would always remain unpleasant. Men could be attracted into these by higher pay or shorter hours, instead of being driven into them by destitution. The community would then have a strong economic motive for finding ways of diminishing the disagreebleness of these exceptional trades.

There would still have to be money, or something analogous to it, in any community such as we are imagining. The Anarchist plan of a free distribution of the total produce of work in equal shares does not get rid of the need for some standard of exchange value, since one man will choose to take his share in one form and another in another. When the day comes for distributing luxuries, old ladies will not want their quota of cigars, nor young men their just proportion of lap-dog; this will make it necessary to know how many cigars are the equivalent of one lap-dog. Much the simplest way is to pay an income, as at present, and allow relative values to be adjusted according to demand. But if actual coin were paid, a man might hoard it and in time become a capitalist. To prevent this, it would be best to pay notes available only during a certain period, say one year from the date of issue. This would enable a man to save up for his annual holiday, but not to save indefinitely.

There is a very great deal to be said for the Anarchist plan of allowing necessaries, and all commodities that can easily be produced in quantities adequate to any possible demand, to be given away freely to all who ask for them, in any amounts they may require. The question whether this plan should be adopted is, to my mind, a purely technical one: would it be, in fact, possible to adopt it without much waste and consequent diversion of labor to the production of necessaries when it might be more usefully employed otherwise? I have not the means of answering this question, but I think it exceedingly probable that, sooner or later, with the continued improvement in the methods of production, this Anarchist plan will become feasible; and when it does, it certainly ought to be adopted.

Women in domestic work, whether married or unmarried, will receive pay as they would if they were in industry. This will secure the complete economic independence of wives, which is difficult to achieve in any other way, since mothers of young children ought not to be expected to work outside the home.

The expense of children will not fall, as at present, on the parents. They will receive, like adults, their share of necessaries, and their education will be free.[1] There is no longer to be the present competition for scholarships among the abler children: they will not be imbued with the competitive spirit from infancy, or forced to use their brains to an unnatural degree with consequent listlessness and lack of health in later life. Education will be far more diversified than at present; greater care will be taken to adapt it to the needs of different types of young people. There will be more attempt to encourage initiative young pupils, and less desire to fill their minds with a set of beliefs and mental habits regarded as desirable by the State, chiefly because they help to preserve the *status quo*. For the great majority of children it will probably be found desirable to have much more outdoor education in the country. And for older boys and girls whose interests are not intellectual or artistic, technical education, undertaken in a liberal spirit, is far more useful in promoting mental activity than book-learning which they regard (however falsely) as wholly useless except for purposes of examination. The really useful educa-

---

[1] Some may fear that the result would be an undue increase of population, but such fears I believe to be groundless. See above, Chapter IV, on "Work and Pay." Also, Chapter vi of "Principles of Social Reconstruction" (George Allen and Unwin, Ltd.).

tion is that which follows the direction of the child's own instinctive interests, supplying knowledge for which it is seeking, not dry, detailed information wholly out of relation to its spontaneous desires.

Government and law will still exist in our community, but both will be reduced to a minimum. There will still be acts which will be forbidden—for example, murder. But very nearly the whole of that part of the criminal law which deals with property will have become obsolete, and many of the motives which now produce murders will be no longer operative. Those who nevertheless still do commit crimes will not be blamed or regarded as wicked; they will be regarded as unfortunate, and kept in some kind of mental hospital until it is thought that they are no longer a danger. By education and freedom and the abolition of private capital the number of crimes can be made exceedingly small. By the method of individual curative treatment it will generally be possible to secure that a man's first offense shall also be his last, except in the case of lunatics and the feeble-minded, for whom of course a more prolonged but not less kindly detention may be necessary.

Government may be regarded as consisting of two parts: the one, the decisions of the community or its recognized organs; the other, the enforcing of those decisions upon all who resist them. The first part is not objected to by Anarchists. The second part, in an ordinary civilized State, may remain entirely in the background: those who have resisted a new law while it was being debated will, as a rule, submit to it when it is passed, because resistance is generally useless in a settled and orderly community. But the possibility of governmental force remains, and indeed is the very reason for the submission which makes force unnecessary. If, as Anarchists desire, there were no use of force by government, the majority could still band themselves together and use force against the minority. The only difference would be that their army or their police force would be *ad hoc*, instead of being permanent and professional. The result of this would be that everyone would have to learn how to fight, for fear a welldrilled minority should seize power and establish an old-fashioned oligarchic State. Thus the aim of the Anarchists seems hardly likely to be achieved by the methods which they advocate.

The reign of violence in human affairs, whether within a country or in its external relations, can only be prevented, if we have not been mistaken, by an authority able to declare all use of force except by itself illegal, and strong enough to be obviously capable of making all other use of force futile, except when it could secure the support of public opinion as a defense of freedom or a resistance to injustice. Such an authority exists within a country: it is the

State. But in international affairs it remains to be created. The difficulties are stupendous, but they must be overcome if the world is to be saved from periodical wars, each more destructive than any of its predecessors. Whether, after this war, a League of Nations will be formed, and will be capable of performing this task, it is as yet impossible to foretell. However that may be, some method of preventing wars will have to be established before our Utopia becomes possible. When once men *believe* that the world is safe from war, the whole difficulty will be solved: there will then no longer be any serious resistance to the disbanding of national armies and navies, and the substitution for them of a small international force for protection against uncivilized races. And when that stage has been reached, peace will be virtually secure.

The practice of government by majorities, which Anarchists criticise, is in fact open to most of the objections which they urge against it. Still more objectionable is the power of the executive in matters vitally affecting the happiness of all, such as peace and war. But neither can be dispensed with suddenly. There are, however, two methods of diminishing the harm done by them: (1) Government by majorities can be made less oppressive by devolution, by placing the decision of questions primarily affecting only a section of the community in the hands of that section, rather than of a Central Chamber. In this way, men are no longer forced to submit to decisions made in a hurry by people mostly ignorant of the matter in hand and not personally interested. Autonomy for internal affairs should be given, not only to areas, but to all groups, such as industries or Churches, which have important common interests not shared by the rest of the community. (2) The great powers vested in the executive of a modern State are chiefly due to the frequent need of rapid decisions, especially as regards foreign affairs. If the danger of war were practically eliminated, more cumbrous but less autocratic methods would be possible, and the Legislature might recover many of the powers which the executive has usurped. By these two methods, the intensity of the interference with liberty involved in government can be gradually diminished. Some interference, and even some danger of unwarranted and despotic interference, is of the essence of government, and must remain so long as government remains. But until men are less prone to violence than they are now, a certain degree of governmental force seems the lesser of two evils. We may hope, however, that if once the danger of war is at an end, men's violent impulses will gradually grow less, the more so as, in that case, it will be possible to diminish enormously the individual power which now makes rulers autocratic and ready for almost any act of tyranny in order to crush opposition. The development of a world where even governmental force has become unnecessary (except against lunatics) must be gradual. But as a gradual process it is perfectly possible; and when it has been completed we may hope to see the principles of Anarchism embodied in the management of communal affairs.

How will the economic and political system that we have outlined bear on the evils of character? I believe the effect will be quite extraordinarily beneficent.

The process of leading men's thought and imagination away from the use of force will be greatly accelerated by the abolition of the capitalist system, provided it is not succeeded by a form of State Socialism in which officials have enormous power. At present, the capitalist has more control over the lives of others than any man ought to have; his friends have authority in the State; his economic power is the pattern for political power. In a world where all men and women enjoy economic freedom, there will not be the same habit of command, nor, consequently, the same love of despotism; a gentler type of character than that now prevalent will gradually grow up. Men are formed by their circumstances, not born ready-made. The bad effect of the present economic system on character, and the immensely better effect to be expected from communal ownership, are among the strongest reasons for advocating the change.

In the world as we have been imagining it, economic fear and most economic hope will be alike removed out of life. No one will be haunted by the dread of poverty or driven into ruthlessness by the hope of wealth. There will not be the distinction of social classes which now plays such an immense part in life. The unsuccessful professional man will not live in terror lest his children should sink in the scale; the aspiring employe will not be looking forward to the day when he can become a sweater in his turn. Ambitious young men will have to dream other daydreams than that of business success and wealth wrung out of the ruin of competitors and the degradation of labor. In such a world, most of the nightmares that lurk in the background of men's minds will no longer exist; on the other hand, ambition and the desire to excel will have to take nobler forms than those that are encouraged by a commercial society. All those activities that really confer benefits upon mankind will be open, not only to the fortunate few, but to all who have sufficient ambition and native aptitude. Science, labor-saving inventions, technical progress of all kinds, may be confidently expected to flourish far more than at present, since they will be the road to honor, and honor will have to replace money among those of the young who desire to achieve success. Whether art will flourish in a Socialistic community depends upon the form of Socialism adopted; if the State, or any public authority (no matter what), insists upon controlling art, and only licensing those whom it regards as proficient, the result will be disaster. But if there is real freedom, allowing every man who so desires to take up an artist's career at the cost of some sacrifice of comfort, it is likely that the atmosphere of hope, and the absence of economic compulsion, will lead to a much smaller waste of talent than is involved in our present system, and to a much less degree of crushing of impulse in the mills of the struggle for life.

When elementary needs have been satisfied, the serious happiness of most men depends upon two things: their work, and their human relations. In the world that we have been picturing, work will be free, not excessive, full of the interest that belongs to a collective enterprise in which there is rapid progress, with something of the delight of creation even for the humblest unit. And in human relations the gain will be just as great as in work. The only human relations that have value are those that are rooted in mutual freedom, where there is no domination and no slavery, no tie except affection, no economic or conventional necessity to preserve the external show when the inner life is dead. One of the most horrible things about commercialism is the way in which it poisons the relations of men and women. The evils of prostitution are generally recognized, but, great as they are, the effect of economic conditions on marriage seems to me even worse. There is not infrequently, in marriage, a suggestion of purchase, of acquiring a woman on condition of keeping her in a certain standard of material comfort. Often and often, a marriage hardly differs from prostitution except by being harder to escape from. The whole basis of these evils is economic. Economic causes make marriage a matter of bargain and contract, in which affection is quite secondary, and its absence constitutes no recognized reason for liberation. Marriage should be a free, spontaneous meeting of mutual instinct, filled with happiness not unmixed with a feeling akin to awe: it should involve that degree of respect of each for the other that makes even the most trifling interference with liberty an utter impossibility, and a common life enforced by one against the will of the other an unthinkable thing of deep horror. It is not so that marriage is conceived by lawyers who make settlements, or by priests who give the name of " sacrament " to an institution which pretends to find something sanctifiable in the brutal lusts or drunken cruelties of a legal husband. It is not in a spirit of freedom that marriage is conceived by most men and women at present: the law makes it an opportunity for indulgence of the desire to interfere, where each submits to some loss of his or her own liberty, for the pleasure of curtailing the liberty of the other. And the atmosphere of private property makes it more difficult than it otherwise would be for any better ideal to take root.

It is not so that human relations will be conceived when the evil heritage of economic slavery has ceased to mold our instincts. Husbands and wives, parents and children, will be only held together by affection: where that has died, it will be recognized that nothing worth preserving is left. Because affection will be free, men and women will not find in private life an outlet and stimulus to the love of domineering, but all that is creative in their love will have the freer scope. Reverence for whatever makes the soul in those who are loved will be less rare than it is now: nowadays, many men love their wives in the way in which they love mutton, as something to devour and destroy. But in the love that goes with reverence there is a joy of quite another order than any to be found by mastery, a joy which satisfies the spirit and not only the instincts; and satisfaction of instinct and spirit at once is necessary to a happy life, or indeed to any existence that is to bring out the best impulses of which a man or woman is capable.

In the world which we should wish to see, there will be more joy of life than in the drab tragedy of modern every-day existence. After early youth, as things are, most men are bowed down by forethought, no longer capable of light-hearted gaiety, but only of a kind of solemn jollification by the clock at the appropriate hours. The advice to "become as little children" would be good for many people in many respects, but it goes with another precept, "take no thought for the morrow," which is hard to obey in a competitive world. There is often in men of science, even when they are quite old, something of the simplicity of a child: their absorption in abstract thought has held them aloof from the world, and respect for their work has led the world to keep them alive in spite of their innocence. Such men have succeeded in living as all men ought to be able to live; but as things are, the economic struggle makes their way of life impossible for the great majority.

What are we to say, lastly, of the effect of our projected world upon physical evil? Will there be less illness than there is at present? Will the produce of a given amount of labor be greater? Or will population press upon the limits of subsistence, as Malthus taught in order to refute Godwin's optimism?

I think the answer to all these questions turns, in the end, upon the degree of intellectual vigor to be expected in a community which has done away with the spur of economic competition. Will men in such a world become lazy and apathetic? Will they cease to think? Will those who do think find themselves confronted with an even more impenetrable wall of unreflecting conservatism than that which confronts them at present? These are important questions; for it is ultimately to science that mankind must look for their success in combating physical evils.

If the other conditions that we have postulated can be realized, it seems almost certain that there must be less illness than there is at present. Population will no longer be congested in slums; children will have far more of fresh air and open country; the hours of work will be only such as are wholesome, not excessive and exhausting as they are at present.

As for the progress of science, that depends very largely upon the degree of intellectual liberty existing in the new society. If all science is organized and supervised by the State, it will rapidly become stereotyped and dead. Fundamental advances will not be made, because, until they have been made, they will seem too doubtful to warrant the expenditure of public money upon them. Authority will be in the hands of the old, especially of men who have achieved scientific eminence; such men will be hostile to those among the young who do not flatter them by agreeing with their theories. Under a bureaucratic State Socialism it is to be feared that science would soon cease to be progressive and acquired a medieval respect for authority.

But under a freer system, which would enable all kinds of groups to employ as many men of science as they chose, and would allow the " vagabond's wage " to those who desired to pursue some study so new as to be wholly unrecognized, there is every reason to think that science would flourish as it has never done hitherto.[1] And, if that were the case, I do not believe that any other obstacle would exist to the physical possibility of our system.

The question of the number of hours of work necessary to produce general material comfort is partly technical, partly one of organization. We may assume that there would no longer be unproductive labor spent on armaments, national defense, advertisements, costly luxuries for the very rich, or any of the other futilities incidental to our competitive system. If each industrial guild secured for a term of years the advantages, or part of the advantages, of any new invention or methods which it introduced, it is pretty certain that every encouragement would be given to technical progress. The life of a discoverer or inventor is in itself agreeable: those who adopt it, as things are now, are seldom much actuated by economic motives, but rather by the interest of the work together with the hope of honor; and these motives would operate more widely than they do now, since fewer people would be prevented from obeying them by economic necessities. And there is no doubt that intellect would work more keenly and creatively in a world where instinct was less thwarted, where the

---

[1] See the discussion of this question in the preceding chapter.

joy of life was greater, and where consequently there would be more vitality in men than there is at present.

There remains the population question, which, ever since the time of Malthus, has been the last refuge of those to whom the possibility of a better world is disagreeable. But this question is now a very different one from what it was a hundred years ago. The decline of the birth-rate in all civilized countries, which is pretty certain to continue, whatever economic system is adopted, suggests that, especially when the probable effects of the war are taken into account, the population of Western Europe is not likely to increase very much beyond its present level, and that of America is likely only to increase through immigration. Negroes may continue to increase in the tropics, but are not likely to be a serious menace to the white inhabitants of temperate regions. There remains, of course, the Yellow Peril; but by the time that begins to be serious it is quite likely that the birth-rate will also have begun to decline among the races of Asia. If not, there are other means of dealing with this question; and in any case the whole matter is too conjectural to be set up seriously as a bar to our hopes. I conclude that, though no certain forecast is possible, there is not any valid reason for regarding the possible increase of population as a serious obstacle to Socialism.

Our discussion has led us to the belief that the communal ownership of land and capital, which constitutes the characteristic doctrine of Socialism and Anarchist Communism, is a necessary step toward the removal of the evils from which the world suffers at present and the creation of such a society as any humane man must wish to see realized. But, though a necessary step, Socialism alone is by no means sufficient. There are various forms of Socialism: the form in which the State is the employer, and all who work receive wages from it, involves dangers of tyranny and interference with progress which would make it, if possible, even worse than the present *régime*. On the other hand, Anarchism, which avoids the dangers of State Socialism, has dangers and difficulties of its own, which make it probable that, within any reasonable period of time, it could not last long even if it were established. Nevertheless, it remains an ideal to which we should wish to approach as nearly as possible, and which, in some distant age, we hope may be reached completely. Syndicalism shares many of the defects of Anarchism, and, like it, would prove unstable, since the need of a central government would make itself felt almost at once.

The system we have advocated is a form of Guild Socialism, leaning more, perhaps, towards Anarchism than the official Guildsman would wholly approve. It is in the matters that politicians usually ignore—

science and art, human relations, and the joy of life—that Anarchism is strongest, and it is chiefly for the sake of these things that we included such more or less Anarchist proposals as the "vagabond's wage." It is by its effects outside economics and politics, at least as much as by effects inside them, that a social system should be judged. And if Socialism ever comes, it is only likely to prove beneficent if non-economic goods are valued and consciously pursued.

The world that we must seek is a world in which the creative spirit is alive, in which life is an adventure full of joy and hope, based rather upon the impulse to construct than upon the desire to retain what we possess or to seize what is possessed by others. It must be a world in which affection has free play, in which love is purged of the instinct for domination, in which cruelty and envy have been dispelled by happiness and the unfettered development of all the instincts that build up life and fill it with mental delights. Such a world is possible; it waits only for men to wish to create it.

Meantime, the world in which we exist has other aims. But it will pass away, burned up in the fire of its own hot passions; and from its ashes will spring a new and younger world, full of fresh hope, with the light of morning in its eyes.

George, Lloyd, 156
German Communist League, 5
German Working Men's Association, 5
Germany, 144
Giles, Lionel, 35 n.
God and the State, 48
Godwin, 207
Gompers, 76
Gospels, The, 187
Government, 111 ff., 198 ff.
  representative, 117, 129 ff., 137 ff.
Guesde, Jules, 59-60
Guild Congress, 83, 134 ff., 194
Guild Socialism, xi, 80 ff., 133, 192, 211
  and the State, 82-4, 114, 184-5
Guillaume, James, 36 n., 37

Haywood, 77
Hegel, 4
Herd instinct, xv
Heubner, 41
History, materialistic interpretation of, 7
Hobson, J. A., 140
Hodgskin, 5 n.
Hulme, T. E., 29
Hypocrisy, 132

Idleness, 103 ff.
Independent Labor Party, 57
India, 158
Individual 138

Industrial Relations, American Commission on, 78
Industrial Workers of the World (I.W.W.), xi, 31, 74
International alliance of socialist democracy, 44
International fraternity, 43
International Working Men's Association, 6, 44 ff., 59
Internationalism, 148, 150

Japan, 151
Jaurès, 60
Jouhaux, 75
Joy of Life, 206

Keats, 173
Knowledge, 165
Kropotkin, 36, 46, 50-51, 87 ff., 96 n., 100 n., 102, 106 n., 116 ff., 179, 192
Kultur, 159

Labor, integration of, 92
Labor Party, 57, 150
Lagardelle, 64
Law, 111 ff., 198
Levine, Louis, 59 n., 60 n.
Liberal Party, 28, 30
Liberty, 33, 111 ff., 192, 201
  and syndicalism, 85
  and anarchism, 108
  and creative impulse, 169, 172-81
  and art, 182-3, 204
  and human relations, 204

INDEX

Liquor Traffic, 137
Livre, Fédération du, 178
Lunatics, 119
Lynching, 122

Magistrates, 101
Majorities, divine right of, 130, 200
Malthus, 86 ff., 207 ff.
Manchesterism, 29
Marriage, 204
Marx, x, 1-31, 36, 60, 77, 148, 164
    biography, 3-7
    doctrines, 7-31, 113
    and Bakunin, 38 ff.
    and International Working Men's Association, 44 ff., 59 *n.*
Marxisme, La décomposition du, 29
Mazzini, 43
Millennium by force, 131, 164
Millerand, 60, 61
Milton, 173
Miners, Western Federation of, 76, 78
Money, 195
Monroe Doctrine, 140
Morning Star, 21
Morris, William, 175

Napoleon, 120
Napoleon III, 46
Naquet, Alfred, 98 *n.*, 118 *n.*, 165

National Guilds, 81 *n.*
National Guilds League, 82
Nationalism, 17, 25, 28, 32
Nations—
    relations of, 139 ff.
    League of, 132, 200
Necessaries, free? 109, 196
Neue Reinische Zeitung, 41
Nicholas, Tsar, 43

Opera Singers, 195
Opium Traffic, 137
Orage, 81 *n.*
Owen, Robert, 5 *n.*

Pellico, Silvio, 42
Pelloutier, 54, 63
Permeation, 57
Persia, 158
Plato, vii
Poets, 104
Poland, 37, 144
Population, 197 *n.*
Possibilists, 60
Poverty, 190
Power, love of, 111, 144, 160, 161
Press, 143
Production, methods of, 87 ff.
Proletariat, 11 ff.
Proportional Representation, 155
Proudhon, 4 *n.*, 38
Pugnacity, 147
Punishment, 123 ff.

Ravachol, 53

INDEX

Ravenstone, Piercy, 5 *n*.
Reclue, Elisée, 48 *n*.
Revisionism, 27, 56
Revolution—
  French, 7
  Russian, 18, 67, 148, 154
  Social, 6, 17, 70, 113, 148, 154, 164
  of 1848, 3, 5, 40
Ruge, 38

Sabotage, 66
Saint-Simon, 4 *n*.
Sand, George, 38, 41
Sarajevo, 32
Scholarships, 170, 197
Science, 86, 109, 138 166 ff., 189, 207
  men of, 207
Self-interest, 125
Sharing, free, 96 ff., 195
Shelley, 173
Single Tax, 82
Slavery, 190
Socialism, *passim*—
  defined, 1
  English, 5
  French, 4, 59
  German, 56
  evolutionary, 27
  State, 57, 107, 115, 128, 170, 174, 202, 208
  and distribution, 93 ff.
  and art and science, 164 ff., 203
  Guild, *see* Guild Socialism

Socialist Labor Party, 76
Socialist Revolutionaries, Alliance of, 43
Socialists, Inter-Allied, 156
Sorel, 29, 67
Spinoza, 120
State, x, xi, 1, 16, 30, 48, 60, 68, 78, 82-4, 107 ff., 138, 145
Strikes, 66, 67, 70, 78 ff., 130
Syndicalism, *passim*—
  and Marx, 28, 115
  and party, 30
  and liberty, 85
  and political action, 30, 69 129 ff.
  and anarchism, x, 55, 72, 115
  in France, 58 ff.
  in Italy, 58 *n*.
  reformist and revolutionary, 62
  and class-war, 65, 115
  and general strike, 67, 69, 130
  and the State, 68, 115
  and Guild Socialism, 81 *n*., 134
Syndicalist Railwayman, 69
Syndicats, 65

Tariffs, 137
Technical Training, 169 ff., 197
Theft, 121
Thompson, William, 5 *n*.
Tolstoy, 32

INDEX

Trade Unionism, x, 13, 62
   industrial, 31, 74 ff.
   craft, 73
Trusts, 75, 141

Utopias, vii, 3, 200

Vagabond's wage, 177, 193, 208, 212
Villeneuves Saint Georges, 71
Violence, crimes of, 121, 122, 199
Violence, Reflections on, 29
Viviani, 60
Volkstimme, 27 *n.*
Volunteers, 121

Wages, 2, 78, 93 ff., 192
   iron law of, 26
   and art and science, 168 ff.

Wagner, Richard, 41
Waldeck-Rousseau, 61, 63
Walkley, Mary Anne, 20
War—
   avoidance of, 139 ff., 199
   and capitalism, 139 ff.
   and the Press 143 ff.
Women—
   votes for, 155
   economic independence of, 196
Work—
   and wages, 93 ff., 194
   hours of, 102, 193, 209
   can it be made pleasant? 100, 193, 204

Yellow races, 151, 210

THE SOCIALISM OF TO-DAY

Edited by

WILLIAM ENGLISH WALLING, JESSIE WALLACE HUGHAN,
J. G. PHELPS STOKES, HARRY W. LAIDLER, and
other members of a committee of the
Intercollegiate Socialist Society

630 pages, 12mo, $1.75 net

This volume is the first comprehensive source book on the International Socialist movement ever published. It consists chiefly of original documents—speeches, programs, platforms, articles by noted Socialists and Socialist organizations all over the world.

"The publication of this book marks a distinct advance in the scientific discussion of the Socialist movement."—*Review of Reviews*

"The present work aims to present in a rigidly impartial way a documentary description of the Socialist movement. No such comprehensive source book has yet appeared. Invaluable as a work of reference, it removes any excuse for ignorance of what organized Socialism stands for."—PROFESSOR R. C. MCCREA, in the *Annals of the American Academy*.

"As a compact, inclusive summary of the significant literature of the subject, there is nothing equal to it in English."—*Christian Science Monitor*.

" The Socialism of To-day' is an encyclopedia. It should be in every Socialist library. Our writers, speakers and young Socialists ought to use it constantly. Let us begin to know."—DR. WILLIAM E. BOHN, in *International Socialist Review*.

HENRY HOLT AND COMPANY
PUBLISHERS   NEW YORK